A TASTE OF JOY AND LIBERTY

A TASTE OF JOY AND LIBERTY

A Philosopher Encounters the Gospel of Jesus

Jeffrey Wattles

ORIGIN PRESS

www.OriginPress.org
Copyright © 2025 by Jeffrey Wattles

Cover design by BookDesigners.com

All rights reserved. This book is protected by copyright.

No part of it may be reproduced, stored in a retrieval system, or transmitted in any form or by any means, electronic, mechanical, photocopying, recording, or otherwise without written permission from the author.

ISBN: 978-1-57983-064-9 (paperback)
eISBN: 978-1-57983-067-0 (eBook)

Printed in the United States of America

First printing: August 2025

Contents

Preface vii

Part I
THE HUMAN JESUS GROWS TO FULL MATURITY AND LAUNCHES HIS PUBLIC MINISTRY

1 | Introduction 3
2 | The Historical Jesus 9
3 | The Saving Faith of a Little Child 19
4 | The Kingdom of God Within You 33
5 | Jesus's Scientific Knowledge 45
6 | Developing Righteous Character 55
7 | Finding God's Will 65
8 | Jesus at Age Twelve 79
9 | The Decisions That Launched Jesus's Public Ministry 87
10 | Finding Joy in Life 99

Part II
THE SON OF MAN TEACHES HIS ORIGINAL MESSAGE

11 | How Jesus Taught Living Truth 109
12 | The Living Truth of the Kingdom of God and the Family of God 117
13 | Revealing God as Father and Mother 127
14 | Loving God and the Neighbor Wholeheartedly 139
15 | Being Merciful and Forgiving 155
16 | Doing Good to Others 167

Part III
THE SON OF GOD REVEALS HIS DIVINITY

17 | Responding to Different Levels of Hostility   183
18 | The Advanced Level of Jesus's Gospel   193
19 | Forceful Peacemaker   203
20 | How Jesus Led His Followers into Spiritual Unity   211
21 | How Jesus Interpreted His Death on the Cross   221

Part IV
THE RESURRECTED JESUS CONTINUES HIS WORK THROUGH US

22 | Resurrection in This Life and the Next   233
23 | What the Spirit Does—and Does Not Do—for Us   239
24 | Hope for a Much Better World Coming Soon   245
25 | Jesus and His Gospel: The Agenda   253

Acknowledgments   263
Further Reading   265
Endnotes   266
List of Abbreviations   269

Preface

My childhood spiritual experience began at age four—was it in a dream?—with a realization of the spirit of God pervading the Sunday school classroom. On my sixth birthday, after blowing out the candles on the cake, I was asked what I wished for. I softly revealed my evangelistic heart: "I want everyone to know Jesus." By then, I would rise early in the mornings and go to the family room before everyone else was up. I would read the Bible, often with tears. I especially recall being moved by the Book of Matthew. At one point when I was seven, I looked up to heaven and dedicated myself to the quest for perfection.

I was sixteen when I started to discover truth, beauty, and goodness as a trio of bright, calm, luminous spiritual values—which I came to realize were also present in Jesus. At twenty-six, after an undergraduate philosophy degree at Stanford, then as a philosophy graduate student at Northwestern University, I committed myself to integrating all these inputs to help form a new philosophy of living. Science, philosophy, spiritual experience, natural beauty, aesthetics, ethics—all were essential.

At the same time, I came to see *the gospel as the spiritual crown of the new philosophy.* The gospel has many aspects to it, but one pair of aspects struck me in particular: the concept of God as a loving and merciful Father and humankind as a universal family.

I did extra study for a year at Fuller Theological Seminary and two years in religious studies including some teaching in the University of Toronto. In evangelism, when I go door-to-door, I say: "I'm your neighbor, Jeff, encouraging you in the faith that you are a son or daughter of God." I smile, fall silent, and let the conversation go forward from there. I often ask Christians what it means to them to be a daughter or son of God. I volunteered for ten years with an evangelistic group answering listener mail from around the world as part of a radio broadcast ministry. When I would give a talk, I would often close by saying, "Always know that you are a divinely created, infinitely loved, spiritually indwelt, evolutionary, free-will, son or daughter of God!"

My commitment to the gospel as a trained philosopher led me to specialize in the golden rule of treating others as you want others to do to you. Oxford University Press published my book, *The Golden Rule* (1996). My mature philosophy is set forth in *Living in Truth, Beauty, and Goodness* (Cascade, 2016). When this book was off to the publisher, I was planning to dedicate my life to teaching the new philosophy that I describe in that book.

But within a few months, I became aware of being drawn to some specifically spiritual project. I went to speak with a prophetic minister whose sermons I had always found insightful. He had read my second book and called me to write a third one, building on the sections on Jesus in the second one. At this point in my life, writing another book was the last thing on my mind.

Nevertheless, after a few weeks, in a dream, I reconnected with a project that I had long honored. My book would promote a planetary spiritual renaissance by helping followers of Jesus come to know him and his gospel better. Working on each chapter, I had to grow in relation to the topic and apply the lessons in my life before I could get the clarity needed to finish the chapter.

As a basis for these activities, I have been fortunate to have taught a broad range of subjects, worked in a great variety of jobs, and traveled widely. At an international school in Berkeley, California, I taught world history, world religions, world literature, public speaking, business case analysis, and more. In addition, mostly at Kent State University, I have led over three thousand students through experiential projects that integrated academic progress with holistic personal growth. And I would always do projects with each class.

Moreover, with varying degrees of seriousness, I have worked as a fry cook, as an accounting clerk, in a factory, in many sales positions, as a guitar teacher and musical entertainer, and in academic administration. Travels, study, evangelism, work, and family have taken me to Israel, Turkey, Greece, Italy, Spain, Germany, Austria, France, the Netherlands, Belgium, Switzerland, Hungary, Bulgaria, Finland, Denmark, Estonia, England, Australia, New Zealand, Bali (Indonesia), Canada, Mexico, Colombia, Senegal, China, and Japan.

My wife is a strong, caring, funny, practical genius who grew up as a rural Japanese woman; and our son is a spiritually sensitive, friendly, successful businessman who is married and lives in Tokyo.

Part I

HOW THE HUMAN JESUS DEVELOPED HIS CHARACTER

Through his life and teachings, Jesus revealed God and showed how a human child of God can do God's will on earth as it is done in heaven. We, too, can learn to do these things.

The first part of Jesus's mission was to grow up from childhood to full maturity. He developed a character that was strong, well-balanced, and centered in God. The steps of growth that are set forth in Part I illustrate how every believer can become like Jesus as we grow up with him and achieve a character like his.

Because I regard many of Jesus's teachings as implicitly autobiographical, I use his later teachings to present an idea of his younger years. I believe that he found God by faith as a little child, and that, by his late twenties, he had discovered most of his original, basic, saving gospel.

In Part I, after some historical background, we focus in chapter 3 on becoming spirit-born. Then we build—God builds—on that foundation.

1

Introduction

JESUS OF NAZARETH knew God better than any other person did who has ever walked this earth. No wonder so many people are drawn to him and his teachings.

But how many of us truly know Jesus? And what was the gospel that he lived and taught?

Most of all, this book aims to help the reader get to know Jesus and his gospel better. These goals are achieved by:

- Relating with him personally

- Understanding what he proclaimed as the Son of Man: his original saving message of the kingdom of God and the family of God

- Grasping his full, advanced gospel, including his divinity as the Son of God

- Learning to live his teachings and acquiring a character like his

To meet these needs, this book offers a new perspective on the life and teachings of Jesus. The four parts of this book are designed in rough chronological order, focusing on what I propose as *the four main stages of Jesus's life*. (1) From his birth, he grew up to full human maturity by the time of his baptism. (2) Then he publicly taught his original message. (3) Next, conflict broke out into the open when he began to teach his full gospel; thus began the third period of his life, which lasted all the way to the cross. (4) Since that time, mostly by his spirit, he has continued his work with, in, and through us, bringing hope for a spiritual renaissance and a much better world in this century or the next.

In a secondary way, this book is structured according to four stages of spirituality: spirit-born, spirit-taught, spirit-led, and spirit-filled. I believe that the human Jesus completed all four of these levels by the time he was baptized. But, as we shall see, it also makes sense to link each part of the book to the corresponding spiritual stage.

This linking sustains progress in learning to live Jesus's teachings and in growing up with him. To gain something akin to his maturity involves developing a character like his: strong, wisely balanced, and centered in God.

As we read this book (me, too), Jesus and his gospel will increasingly become more alive in us. Going forward, we do well to select teachings that we want to learn to live or qualities of Jesus that we want to acquire, **as we are realistically able to do so.** Without tackling too much, we take creative steps to find things to do that will enable us to come closer to our personal growth goals. Self-help takes us part of the way, but the real growth is a gift from God.

Let us begin with a word about the relationships between persons interested in this inquiry.

Intellectual Differences and Spiritual Unity

A friend of mine was welcoming a group of incoming seminary students. He told them to stand up with everything they agreed with and sit down with everything they disagreed with. Then he read a short text, phrase by phrase. All around the room, as the students were standing up and sitting down, they saw each other do so in such a chaotic way that everyone burst out laughing.

They were experiencing spiritual unity in the face of their intellectual differences. No one thought that intellectual differences do not matter. But they discovered that laughter can enable divine spirit to put these differences in their place. On this basis, discussion goes forward in a transformed light.

As you read this book, if you find ideas that you would like to work with, you are encouraged to transplant them into the garden of beliefs that you already cherish. We are family, and getting everyone to agree with my language and concepts is not what this book is about. As an author, my dream is for you to deepen your loving communion with Jesus, to better understand and live his teachings, and to share them wisely.

Perhaps the most essential thing that many religions do is to teach about our basic relationship with God and with other persons. Jesus also did this. Searching wholeheartedly to discover his original message, several scholars in the eighteenth and nineteenth centuries began using new historical tools. Some of them broke through to the realization that the heart of Jesus's message was the fatherhood of God and the brotherhood of man. Today, many people would prefer the language of the parenthood of God and the siblinghood of humankind. No matter what words we use, these phrases refer to living spiritual realities. *I will show how this pair of truths can function as the hub around which all other gospel teachings fit.*

Although the fatherhood of God was a pillar of Jesus's gospel two thousand years ago, it remains an open question how we can best express his revelation today. Many people question, struggle with, or reject, the idea of God as a father. Jesus would never have pressured anyone to use a particular name for God. Each person has a unique personal adventure of discovering God, and a story about how they came to their own name(s) for God. Countless wonderfully God-knowing persons have used different names and developed magnificent relationships with the Creator. Each person is free to choose a name for God that fits their discovery of the divine friend who is present within him or her.

The quality of our relationships with God and the neighbor matters far more than the language we use. In every age, eternal truth needs fresh expression to meet the needs of the current generation. In our interactions in the universal family of God, it helps to avoid languageism—looking down on others because of the language that they choose sincerely to express truth as it has become meaningful to them.

This theme of spiritual unity is mostly implicit in Part I, grounded in Part II, dominant in chapter 20, and prominent in chapters 24 and 25.

The Readers I Have in Mind

I write for persons who:

- Are mature Christians who have the time to grow
- Are independent thinkers who are philosophically and spiritually minded

- Hunger for divine connection that brings meaning, purpose, and stability
- Have major questions about Jesus and what he taught
- Would like to be like Jesus
- Are considering becoming a follower of Jesus
- Have not yet found what they are looking for in Christianity
- Belong to other religions or no religion, and want to see whether this presentation of Jesus and his gospel can truly respect persons in other religions as equals in the family of faith

I also write for the unique *you*, no matter what you believe or do not believe, no matter what you are searching for and what you don't like, no matter what you have done or not done. You are a divinely created and infinitely loved child of God. Your divine Parent has sent you a personal gift, the spirit of God to live within you. You have the perfect guide and friend.

Transition

This book takes you on a tour through some of the things that Jesus said and did. It is like riding in a bus in Israel and beyond, visiting some of the places where these things happened. At each site, we get off the bus to see for ourselves, to remember, imagine, and reflect. As tour guide, I have the author's microphone as the bus approaches one sight after another. But chapter by chapter, what is essential is for you to get off the bus, commune, and have your own experience.

2

The Historical Jesus

To BEGIN TO know Jesus of Nazareth (ca. 4–7 BCE to 30 CE), we shall start with some historical background. But this background, according to most historians, is found exclusively through using the tools of academic history. Reconstructing the historical Jesus in this way, we leave out all spiritual meanings, values, and religious beliefs.

However, the phrase "historical Jesus" has another meaning; it also refers to who Jesus really was and what he said and did. But if Jesus really was and is the Son of God, then in order to state the truth, we must use more than historical knowledge; we need faith. When I use the term "historical Jesus," I have both meanings in mind.

At different times in our lives, we ask the question: what is my purpose in life? I have read accounts of "typical" Gen Z young people asking this question; and all kinds of big changes can bring this question to the fore. In the rest of this book, I pay attention to the various things that Jesus said about his mission, which I define as the cluster of the most important tasks that were part of the Father's will for him. The statements that reveal his mission represent aspects of his life purpose. And our particular sense of purpose can flourish by finding aspects of Jesus's mission that we can enter into.

Toward the end of this chapter, I propose a concept of Jesus's mission that is my own. And between the beginning and the end of the chapter is a historical narrative which adds a meaningful framework for Jesus's concept of his own mission, his own purpose in life.

The Broadest Time Perspective

Jesus was wholeheartedly engaged in his mission as the first century unfolded. But he did so with a wisdom that was based on a divine perspective; he looked back into the remote past and forward into the distant future. I believe that Jesus recognized that God is the Lord of history, and the Creator is not in a hurry. A thousand of our years is like a single day from God's perspective (Ps 90:4, 2 Pt 3:8). Jesus developed a perspective which shed light on the basic relationships of God and human beings, as well as his purpose during his life on earth.

Jesus grew up with the Jewish belief that the origin of every human being goes back to the Creator of "the heavens and the earth," who said, "Let us make humans in our own image, according to our likeness" (Gn 1:1, 26).[1]

This idea was imprinted upon Jesus because he was a member of a particular people whose beginning was four thousand years ago. The affirmation of the image of God in all people is expressed in the formal agreement, or covenant, that God made with Abraham to bless him; and through him, "all the families of the earth shall be blessed" (Gn 12:3). This covenant anticipates, in a way, Jesus's offering blessings to all humankind. The offspring of Abraham and his wife Sarah became the Hebrew people, also called Israelites or Jews. The covenant promised God's blessing, and these people were to believe in, and obey, the one God. Jesus formally confirmed his bond with the Jewish people by going to John the Baptist to launch his career as a public teacher (explained in the first three sections of chapter 9).

Jesus revealed our glorious planetary destiny when he prayed, "Your kingdom come, your will be done on earth as in heaven" (Mt 6:10). In other words, when the kingdom of God is fully actualized on earth, people will do God's will in a heavenly way. The human Jesus revealed how a human being can—even now, on this planet—learn to live the will of God in this divinely true, beautiful, and good way.

The Inspiring Leadership of Moses

Around 1700 BCE, during a famine, many of the Hebrews had gone down to Egypt in order to find work and food, only to be taken into slavery. Their oppression persisted for four hundred years, until around 1260, when Moses arose and led them from bondage into freedom.

From place to place, for forty years, Moses led the community that followed him, teaching them about God (Yahweh, often translated as "the Lord"). He gave the people discipline and laws, for example, the Ten Commandments (Ex 20:1–17, Dt 5:6–21): Worship only God, not images. Rest and worship one day a week. Honor your parents. Do not commit murder, theft, or adultery. Do not bear false witness against your neighbor. And do not crave to have for yourself any kind of possession that belongs to your neighbor.

From the teachings of Moses, Jesus chose what he would call "the greatest commandment" and a second one "like it": "You shall love the lord your God we need to insert "with all your heart," so that the sentence reads: "You shall love the Lord your God with all your heart, and with all your soul, and with all your mind, and with all your strength. . . . and with all your soul, and with all your mind, and with all your strength. . . . You shall love your neighbor as yourself" (Dt 6:4, Lv 19:18, Mk 12:28). It was liberating for many people in Jesus's day to embrace the simplicity of this summary of the law. These commandments represented for Jesus the first great step of putting into practice the truths of our basic relationships with God and humans: that God is our Father, and that we are family.

The Monarchy, Its Division, and Lessons That Followed

The early, tribal period continued until, in the eleventh century, a monarchy was established under three kings, Saul, David, and Solomon. At the time of Jesus, people were looking for the Messiah, the "Anointed One," to restore the monarchy and sit on the throne of David. But after Solomon, the kingdom was divided between Judah in the south and Israel in the north.

A conflict between peoples that was important in Jesus's time began in the eighth century BCE, when the Assyrian army took over the Northern Kingdom of Israel, whose capital was Samaria. In addition to its devastating cruelty, Assyria had a policy designed to prevent its conquered peoples from ever rising up again in rebellion, a policy of ethnic mixing. They would deport the priests, people who were educated, and the leadership elite generally, and scatter them into other areas of their kingdom; and then from those areas, they would bring in people to settle in the newly conquered territory. As a result, over centuries, the Israelites who were left in the territory of Samaria blended their genes, customs, and religious beliefs and practices with those of their neighbors. They worshipped Yahweh, the God of Israel, along with tribal gods, which made for religious confusion, in contrast with the Jews, who normally focused their worship on God alone. Samaritans did not regard the Jerusalem Temple as the divinely chosen place for worship; instead, they worshipped on Mount Gerizim. By the time of Jesus, antagonistic relations between Samaritans and Jews had gone on for centuries, and mutual bad feelings were common.

In the sixth century BCE, the kingdom of Judah would be conquered by Babylon, where many Jews were taken into captivity.[2] There the prophet Second Isaiah proclaimed beautiful truths about the goodness of God.[3] Isaiah also assured the people that they would return to their homeland, which happened when Babylonia was conquered by Persia, whose ruler Cyrus respected the customs and religions of the people he conquered. He sent the captives home to rebuild the Temple and restore Jerusalem and their homeland. Despite interference from the Samaritans, the rebuilding went forward, and the prophet Ezra was the leader most responsible for reintroducing traditional law. From the history of the divided kingdom and other sources of knowledge, Jesus taught a warning that has many applications today. "Every kingdom divided against itself is laid waste, and no city or house divided against itself will stand" (Mt 12:25).

From the Book of Isaiah Jesus took one of his several statements of his mission, "The Spirit of the Lord is upon me, because he has anointed me to bring good news to the poor. He has sent me to proclaim release to the captives and recovery of sight to the blind, to set free those who are oppressed, to proclaim the year of the Lord's favor" (Lk 4:18, Is 61:1). Note that Jesus said different things in different situations, unfolding aspects of his own developing concept of his mission.

And in response to the difficulties between Samaritans and Jews, Jesus sought to transform such attitudes. He did this in part by telling his parable about the good Samaritan who cares for the Jew seriously injured on the side of the road (Lk 10:25–37, Jn 4:3–42).[4]

Some Groups That Jesus Dealt With

The pivotal change between the two main parts of Jesus's life and gospel occurs in the crisis of relationships between Jesus and the religious leaders who opposed him.

The *Pharisees*, who traced their intellectual origin back to Ezra, were a religious and political party or sect. By the first century CE, their view of religious life had become the most common one among Jews. Their concept of righteousness came with a theology of their history, which explained why the Jewish people had suffered devastation under Egypt, Assyria, Babylon, Macedon, and Rome. These miseries were said to be caused by God, who was punishing his people for failing to obey his laws. The Pharisees and many others equated the will of God with obeying the law, and then they equated law with the 613 commandments that could be found in the Torah—the first five books of the Hebrew Bible, regarded as the law of Moses. These laws regulate matters ranging from spiritual essentials to minor details. In addition, there was the oral law, developed over the centuries by religious authorities; it was generally regarded as given by God to Moses but not in written form. It included the laws of religious purity, for example, doing no work on the Sabbath day of rest and eating only with persons who were outwardly, religiously pure. There was a stark contrast between the religious teachings of the Pharisees and the quality of the message that Jesus lived and taught.

In addition to the Pharisees, there were other political and religious parties or sects. The *Sadducees* were the aristocratic priests in the Temple in Jerusalem, and they had their own ways of interpreting the law. They were specialists in the Torah; unlike the Pharisees, they did not believe in the resurrection of the dead. The *scribes* were specialists in religious law who performed legal services all through the land; many of them were Pharisees, and some were members of the Sanhedrin, which was the highest ruling body of the Jews, meeting almost daily in the Jerusalem Temple.

Due to social, political, and economic factors, the gap between elites and non-elites was large.[5] The most important political issue in Palestine at the time of Jesus was how to deal with the miseries of living under the power of the Roman empire. The *Herodians* were supporters of King Herod (or possibly his son, Herod Antipas). The *Zealots* (and other similar groups) advocated violence against the soldiers and authorities of the Roman empire. The Zealots preferred a righteous death rather than life in subjugation to a pagan regime.[6]

Divergent Expectations of the Kingdom of God

When Jesus's parents took their newborn into the Jerusalem Temple, one believer praised God for the child. "He is a light to reveal God to the nations, and he is the glory of your people Israel!" (Lk 2:32 NLT).

Astrologers from the East came seeking "the king of the Jews." Learning of this, the brutal and paranoid King Herod jealously sent out soldiers to find and kill the child. Joseph and Mary were informed just in time. They fled to Egypt, where they stayed until Herod died in 4 BCE (Mt 2). Even though Rome provided good roads and the advantages of Greco-Roman culture, there was a constant threat of violence if the Jews were to revolt. In addition, King Herod, his sons, and others used violence in pursuit of their ends.[7]

At this time, there was a widespread hope for, and expectation of, another leader like Moses. He would establish the kingdom of heaven, the reign or rule of God. He would be the Messiah appointed by God. A majority of people thought of him as one who would function as a king and deliver them from being oppressed as part of the Roman empire. Then he would establish Jerusalem as the seat of authority for Israel and the world.

Toward the end of his life, Moses had prayed to God for guidance in selecting his successor, a leader who would be one like himself. He turned over the command of his followers to Joshua, so that his people would not be "like sheep without a shepherd" (Nm 27:17, Dt 18:15, Lk 1:31, Mt 9:36). Joshua would lead them into the promised land. I think it is significant that "Joshua" is how Jesus's name, given by the angel Gabriel, is said in Hebrew (Lk 1:31).

The Jewish people had long hoped, prayed, and suffered for what they called the kingdom of heaven or kingdom of God. Jesus used these phrases in order to communicate with his hearers, since that was what people were generally looking for and what John the Baptist had been proclaiming. But *Jesus usually used terms signifying family relationships to explain his own concept of the kingdom.*

In some ways, the kingdom concept did not fit his message. A king was known primarily in terms of his power; he was a remote figure who had no personal relationship with his subjects. Kings were often angry, vengeful, and violent. In first-century

Palestine, the kingdom idea was easy to misunderstand, since it was linked to the popular longing for a Messiah to lead an army and deliver the Jews from the rule of Rome.

Nevertheless, if Jesus compromised in his choice of this language, he did so wholeheartedly. After all, in the idea of God as king there is a great truth: the sovereignty of God. The Creator structures energy and matter according to laws of nature. The Sovereign commands his creatures to live in accord with the moral law, expressed for example in the golden rule of doing to others as we want others to do to us. And loving God and the neighbor is required for a person to participate on the spiritual level of the family of God, who loves us all.

Jesus's Purpose—and Ours

I believe that the mission of Jesus, as the successor of Moses, was to lead people into a *spiritual* promised land. Which is exactly what he did. This promised land is what Jesus called *the kingdom of God—an umbrella concept comprising his main ideas and ideals.* This concept includes teachings that enable every believer to become and be like him, even though we will always be less perfect.

On the way to our future, we can do great things if we stay in touch with our support: divine fellowship, abundant mercy, and generous patience. We also gain essential support in the social and spiritual life that we experience in vital religious community.

Jesus's perspective about our creation and destiny, together with his knowledge of history, for example, helped him be realistic about the facts of his time and place. For all his heavenly and spiritual ideals, he was always also grounded in a knowledge of earthly and material matters.

We have glimpsed bits of what Jesus knew about the creation and destiny of humankind and the history of his people. Included are the covenant with the one God to bless all peoples of the earth; some highlights of the work and teachings of Moses; the history of the divided monarchy; diverse groups with whom Jesus interacted; differing expectations of the Messiah; and Jesus's purpose for his work on earth.

In significant ways, we can become like Jesus. We can enter into his broad perspective on history and participate in aspects of his mission. And we can contribute to planetary progress both by developing an increasingly heavenly way of living and by doing good to others.

The next chapter explores Jesus's astonishing concept of how we are saved.

Questions and Invitations

- Everyone is divinely created. If this is so, what does it imply? Does the Creator's design include historical process with its ups and downs on the way to a magnificent destiny? Does this design make room for the decisions that we make? Does it include what Jesus called "the kingdom of God within you" (discussed in chapter 4)?

- What factors in your own history have most shaped your perspective?

- Do you take time to learn more about the history of others who are different from you in important ways? If not, would you be willing to consider taking some time to do this? How could you do it?

- What happens when you think of your present activity as fitting into Jesus's universal mission of helping individuals and the planet come a little closer to a spiritual promised land?

3

The Saving Faith of a Little Child

WHAT DOES IT take to be saved, to be born again, to enter the kingdom of God, the family of God? Different people give various answers, but I will not compare and contrast their perspectives. On the whole, I aim to go straight to Jesus and ask him.

Salvation is the pivotal spiritual transformation that can occur in childhood or any later phase of life. I believe that this event happened within Jesus in his early childhood. In our times, people seek transformation in a broad sense rather than salvation in particular. If we urgently need some component of health or psychological well-being, it is common to feel transformed when this need is met. In many cases, this feeling arises partly because God is reinforcing our positive step forward. But there is a kind of transforming that human beings cannot do by themselves. Salvation is given to us by God when we become ready to receive it.

What Jesus thought about any topic may be gathered from his statements, promises, parables, commands, questions, and things that he did. The topic of salvation is an entryway into his original gospel message, and the things he had to say about it all form a meaningful web. I begin with his teaching on how important it is to begin as a little child.

Imagine the scene. Jesus has been engaged in teaching about family life. The next thing we know, mothers are bringing their children for him to touch and bless. Some of his closest disciples start criticizing the mothers for this interruption. The response of Jesus to these disciples was righteous indignation. To them he simply said, "Let the children come to me; do not stop them, for it is to such as these that the kingdom of God belongs. Truly I tell you, whoever does not receive the kingdom of God as a little child will never enter it" (Mk 10:13–16, Lk 18:17). Jesus was pointing out that his critical disciples were themselves acting in a manner inconsistent with being in the kingdom.

After probing the faith of a little child, this chapter considers four more aspects of salvation: the happiness that Jesus promised to those who are poor in spirit—the humble; Jesus's open arms of welcome for those who ask, seek, and knock; being born of the spirit; and repentance. There follow a reflection on living faith and a word about joy.

A note about terminology. When I discuss the kingdom of God and the family of God, I begin by equating the two, and in this chapter, I use these phrases as synonyms. However, the concepts are overlapping but distinct (chapter 12). Even though Jesus spoke often of the kingdom of God, he tended to explain it in the language of family. The language of family fits Jesus better and communicates better today. This explains my choice to define salvation initially in terms of the faith of a child.

The Meaning of a "Little Child"

When the disciples criticized the mothers for bringing their children to Jesus, he taught a requirement for gaining entrance into the kingdom of God. The kingdom is a gift that can only be received in the manner of a little child. Jesus did not define the childlike attitude; but it reasonable to think that at least an open and receptive attitude of faith is required.

I believe that the child's attitude and manner of relating also include humility. On another occasion, when disciples asked who is the greatest in the kingdom, Jesus brought a child into their midst and said, "Whoever becomes humble like this child is the greatest in the kingdom of heaven" (Mt 18:1–5).

Jesus understood that, as children of our heavenly Father, our relationship with God has some features in common with a good relationship between a little child with its earthly parents. Repeatedly, for months, I would get caught up watching the little girl across the street in the front yard with her father. Every few minutes, she would go to her daddy and lift up her arms. He would bend down and gather her up in his arms for a minute or so. She wanted reassurance, and he was trustworthy. This scene was a charming illustration of the truth of relationships in the family of God; and it showed the goodness of one of the most important human virtues, trustworthiness.[8] And trust in God is well placed: "The eternal God is your refuge, and underneath are the everlasting arms" (Dt 33:27 NIV). Jesus's parable of the mustard seed reinforces how comparatively little we are when we enter the kingdom—and how great our prospects are. "The kingdom of heaven is like a mustard seed that someone took and sowed in his field; it is the smallest of all the seeds, but when it has grown it is the greatest of shrubs and becomes a tree, so that the birds of heaven come and make nests in its branches" (Mt 13:31–32).

Implicit Autobiography in Some of Jesus's Teachings

It is plausible that much of what Jesus taught as an adult he had learned through his own prior experience. In speaking of the faith of "a little child," Jesus was also being autobiographical, telling us something about his own early childhood.

The spiritual life of a child is significantly influenced in the home and surrounding society. Jesus's extraordinary mother Mary would have chosen an outstanding husband in Joseph. Thus, Jesus grew up in a home that would have been an excellent place to begin to know God. Among his neighbors in Nazareth, some would have had strong faith, and this would have encouraged faith in this growing and spiritually receptive child. In later childhood, Jesus would have benefited from the local synagogue, where he would have studied the Hebrew scriptures, in which he would have recognized and rejoiced in its gems.

With these supports plus the spirit of God within him (see the next chapter), it is easy to imagine Jesus relating with his heavenly Father and finding in him the source of his greatest joy. He was beginning to experience God's love for him; and it is plausible that he was starting to love God with all his heart, soul, mind, and strength. This could have motivated him to do the Father's will by making good decisions and doing good to others. These childhood experiences may have helped Jesus to associate a variety of meanings with his later concept of the faith of a little child—which he taught to adults.

Humble, Poor in Spirit, Secure, and Happy

I interpret the next teaching of Jesus as helping us understand the faith of a little child as an attitude of humility. "Happy are the poor in spirit, for theirs is the kingdom of heaven" (Mt 5:6, substituting "happy" for "blessed"). Being poor in spirit cannot mean lacking in self-respect or having a bad attitude toward oneself; this would not be meaningful as a requirement for entering the family of God.

I believe that the phrase, "poor in spirit," implies humility. We need to recognize our growth needs. Persons seeking to enter the family of God need some sense of the difference between the Creator Father and the child. Humility can also be defined by contrast. Its opposite is pride (in the sense of hubris), arrogance, or contempt for others; these interfere with good relationships in the kingdom of God.

This teaching of the kingdom belonging to the poor in spirit comes from Jesus's Sermon on the Mount (Mt 5–7). The Son of Man began with a series of promises that are generally called "beatitudes" (Mt 5:3–12). This term comes from the Latin word *beatitudo*, which means "happiness." The first beatitude promises happiness to the poor in spirit and gives them assurance that the kingdom is theirs. Jesus's course in spiritual happiness had eight promises. The gift of the kingdom of heaven includes salvation that encompasses love, forgiveness, and transformation beginning on earth and continuing into everlasting life. The more we realize the meaning of the kingdom, the more we experience the happiness that Jesus promised.

How can it be so easy to gain salvation? Jesus's simplest answers are: "The Father himself loves you." "It is your Father's good pleasure to give you the kingdom" (Jn 16:27, Lk 12:32). Entrance is free to those with the faith of a child. But staying in the kingdom requires growth.

Whenever we are poor in spirit, if we recognize that we are out of alignment with the divine way, and if we mobilize our energy to go back to this beatitude, things change significantly. We can open ourselves and receive once again, even for the zillionth time, the assurance of faith and a relaxing happiness that restores us and puts us back on the path.

Jesus's Open Arms

More of Jesus's wide-open promises are found in the Sermon on the Mount (Mt 5–7). *"Ask, and you will receive; search, and you will find; knock, and the door will be opened for you"* (Mt 7:7). In my opinion, these assurances are given to those who are humbly open and active—persistent seekers. Asking, searching, and knocking have meaning here in the context of approaching and being welcomed into the kingdom of God.

These promises show the striking openness with which Jesus brought people into the family of God by awakening living faith in receptive hearers. They came from the east and west, north and south. He did not initiate them into a system of theology. Instead, he gave direct teaching plus images that evoked the response of the whole person and gave a wide latitude for interpretation. The door opens to a diverse humanity.

Spiritual Receptivity and Rebirth from Above

Without the faith of a little child, spiritual rebirth—which is equivalent to entering the kingdom—cannot take place. Nicodemus came out under cover of darkness to meet Jesus (Jn 3:1–12). He was a Pharisee, very familiar with the laws of Jewish tradition. He was also a member of the Sanhedrin, the highest ruling court of the Jews, which met in the Temple. He was very impressed with Jesus and said to him, "Rabbi, we know that you are a teacher who has come from God; for no one can do these signs that you do unless God is with that person." These "signs" were deeds of power such as healings.

Jesus could have responded to Nicodemus by quoting scriptures and giving enlightening commentary. But Jesus perceived that Nicodemus needed something else. Jesus gave him the frank diagnosis, "No one can see the kingdom of God without being born from above." In contrast to the theme of the little and humble child, the word "above" was a way of referring to heaven. We need to be born from heaven; "the kingdom of God" and "the kingdom of heaven" were interchangeable ways of referring to the same reality. Nicodemus failed to understand this truth because he made the mistake of interpreting Jesus literally. "How can anyone be born after having grown old?" "Can one enter a second time into the mother's womb and be born?"

Jesus replied: "What is born of the flesh is flesh, and what is born of the Spirit is spirit. Do not be astonished that I said to you, 'You must be born from above. The wind blows where it chooses, and you hear the sound of it, but you do not know where it comes from or where it goes. So it is with everyone who is born of the Spirit'" (Jn 3:6–8). "Wind" and "spirit" are both translations of the same Greek word, *pneuma*. Jesus's reply affirms the importance and reality of spiritual experience—sincere relating with God like Jesus probably did as a child. Jesus's reply also acknowledged human limits in spiritual experience.

Then Jesus tried to reach Nicodemus one last time. He spoke of himself as "the Son of Man" who had "descended from heaven." The term "Son of Man" was the mysterious title that

Jesus chose to refer to himself. It underscores the humanity of Jesus; but Jesus was not just *a* human but *the* human. But if he had descended from heaven, he was also more than human. What he communicated to Nicodemus in private, he did not yet proclaim in his gospel to the crowds, and for good reason, as we will see in the first two chapters of Part III.

This conversation did not bear fruit quickly. But eventually Nicodemus did exercise the faith to protest the injustice of the Sanhedrin's judging Jesus without a hearing, and then, after Jesus's death, joining with Joseph of Arimathea in preparing Jesus's body for burial in the tomb (Jn 7:50–51, 19:38–42).

I believe that Jesus responded to Nicodemus in a way that was designed to help him realize his spiritual poverty, his lack of experience in spiritual realities. If he had asked Jesus for spiritual help, or changed direction and begun to search for God wholeheartedly, or knocked on the door of the kingdom, so to speak, in a way that was humbly ready to begin a new life on a new level, Jesus would have welcomed him on the spot.

Jesus's teaching of the need to be reborn is sometimes interpreted as requiring a powerful religious experience. But spiritual growth can progress in a smooth, gradual way; and we can enter kingdom of God (equivalent to the kingdom of heaven) without sensing that any major threshold has been crossed.

Nevertheless, to be born of the spirit implies beginning a new life as a child of God. This requires ongoing, humble openness. If we choose to cooperate, the religion of the spirit will lead us into new ways of thinking, feeling, and doing.

Note that Jesus's message was centered on God. With Nicodemus he implied his divinity, but he never required people to believe in him or to believe anything about him as part of the price of entering the kingdom and gaining salvation. (The important exception is discussed in Part III, chapter 18, in the section on the enduring validity of the original message.)

Repentance, Needed by Some to Enter the Kingdom

Zacchaeus was lost—the kind of person that Jesus was especially drawn to. The story of Zacchaeus demonstrates the power of spiritual transformation to inspire a great decision and action (Lk 19:1–10).

Zacchaeus was living in reverse and needing to repent—to turn his mind around and say 'YES' to God with his life. Being the chief tax collector in the region, his job was to gather the oppressive taxes demanded by the Roman empire; in addition, he had enriched himself greatly by overcharging people. He would have been hated by the Jews in his area.

But he had heard about Jesus, and when he learned that the famous teacher was going to be coming through Jericho, he went out to meet him. But he was short, and the crowd was already lined up, so that he could not see. So he rushed ahead and climbed up into a sycamore tree to be able to see Jesus when he came by. When Jesus saw Zacchaeus, he called Zacchaeus by name and said that he had to stay with him in his home.

When the crowd heard this, some of them criticized Jesus for staying with a sinner. But Zacchaeus was so full of eager expectation that when he saw Jesus and heard what he said that it triggered his faith. After getting down from the tree, he replied, "Look, half of my possessions, Lord, I will give to the poor, and if I have defrauded anyone of anything, I will pay back four times as much."

Then Jesus described this event with the word "salvation" and gave a major statement of his mission. "Today salvation has come to this house . . . The Son of Man came to seek out and to save the lost." Again, the Son of Man is functioning divinely.

Traditionally, only God is a savior, as the prophet Second Isaiah had spoken in the name of God: "There is no other god besides me, a righteous God and a savior; there is no one besides me. Turn to me and be saved, all the ends of the earth!" (Is 45:21–22).

For his salvation, Zacchaeus had the courage to come to Jesus, face his great weakness, and take powerful and generous action. What Zacchaeus needed to do to enter the kingdom family was to actively exercise transforming faith expressed in repentance.

To this story of repentance, I would add a bit. Jesus said, "I have not come to call the righteous but sinners to repentance" (Lk 5:32); and he concludes the parable of the lost sheep: "There will be more joy in heaven over one sinner who repents than over ninety-nine righteous persons who need no repentance" (Lk 15:7). I interpret these teachings to imply that not everyone needs to repent before entering the kingdom of God.

If the righteous do not need to repent, many others do need to do so. I discuss some details of repentance in connection with forgiveness (chapter 15). And once our process of repenting is completed, our challenge is to let go of guilt feelings in cooperation with the transforming grace of divine mercy.

Finally, every person who enters the family of God starts a more direct and upright relationship with God. This makes us more keenly aware of our need to grow. And sooner or later, our own wandering into actions that go against the will of God make it our turn to repent.

Living Faith, Receptive and Active

Mystery surrounds the work of God's spirit in our mind; and how heaven determines when our spiritual birthday occurs is uncertain. But I believe that we can understand something of what is going on.

I conceive of living faith as a never-ending cycle with two phases. The first is *receptive*. We may be primed to find God by parents, friends, and strangers, social media, personal problems, or restless seeking. All kinds of factors can cooperate with God's silent work of grace in the mind.

The time comes when we see and hear a person filled with faith; or we read, ponder, or pray. *A spiritual truth enters the mind, and the spirit of God illuminates it so that the mind intuitively recognizes its truth. It touches us before we have a chance to doubt or reject it.* Later, our trust may falter; we may choose to uproot it. But at least for a time, we are *in synchrony with spirit*.

When we receive a spiritual realization, we can stop and ponder its meaning and allow it to sink in and take root. For example, we can receive the kingdom of God in the sense of receiving our new primary identity: a member in the family of God.

But to complete the process of making God's gift truly our own, we need to act on it. This can happen by moving into the *active* phase of living faith. We *enter* the family of God by beginning to relate on the basis of our new identity as a child of God.

The connection between salvation and faith is clear in the often-repeated teaching, "by grace you have been saved through faith" (Eph 2:8). This means that saving faith is a gift from God; it is not something that we can earn by what we do.

God-given faith comes with unsuspected power. *Active faith* enables us to make truth a part of ourselves, and it *allows divine spirit to do good through us*. Exercising one's faith develops a larger capacity of receptivity and a greater power to act.

When Jesus had occasion to criticize some of his followers by saying, "you of little faith," he wasn't complaining that God hadn't given them enough (Mt 6:30, 8:26, 16:8, 17:20; Mk 9:22–23). Rather, he was telling them that they were not using the power of their gift. When he said to a person, "Your faith has made you well," he was not denying his own healing power, but emphasizing the essential role of the other person's faith (Mk 5:34, Lk 17:19). Acting on faith completes the circuit of divine giving and human receiving.

Only receptive and active faith is living faith. Only living faith is saving faith. And living faith is growing faith.

A Word About Joy (and Transition)

Joy is the topic of chapter 10, and positive emotions in general are treated in chapter 14. But since joy is essential to full spiritual comprehension and motivation, it is good to draw attention to it now.

Noticing and savoring joys allows them to fill and uplift us. We can savor a joy that we look forward to having in the future, one that we are experiencing in the present, and one that we recall from the past. And with a joyful heart, we become free from anxiety regarding our salvation.

The aspects of salvation that we have explored are sources of joy. The humble faith of a little child, the happiness of a beatitude, Jesus's open arms, repentance—indeed everything that liberates us from some obstacle that stands in the way of our entering into, or progressing in, the family of God—is inherently joyous.

All the blessings that have been mentioned in this chapter are possible because the Father loves us and takes pleasure in giving us the kingdom. If, as I believe, God is love (1 Jn 4:16), then love is so central, so all-pervading and dominant in God that everything that our Parent does expresses love, as does every quality we discern in relating with God. In one way or another, all our joys are bound up with the outworkings of the love of God.

Spiritual rebirth is a milestone on the path of living faith. Whether we enter the kingdom of God dramatically and suddenly, or hardly notice any significant change, spiritual rebirth adds to our joy.

But after we enter the family of God, what comes next? The child grows up to be like the Parent.

The faith of a child makes it easy to enter the family of God, but staying in it requires ongoing growth. To get through the trials and testing that are part of life, we continue to need this same living and growing faith. We are each still a child of God. The Son of Man encourages us with a promise that brings more joy. "Come to me, all you who are weary and are carrying heavy burdens, and I will give you rest. Take my yoke upon you, and learn from me, for I am gentle and humble in heart, and you will find rest for your souls. *For my yoke is easy, and my burden is light*" (Mt 11:28–30).

If we are toiling on one or more big tasks, we may feel like an ox wearing a heavy yoke, pulling a plough all alone through dry, hard, rocky ground. If so, we need to exchange this yoke for another one that two workers can pull together. Not only does Jesus give us an agenda—the will of God—that is manageable. Jesus's companionship also brings new energies, joy, and refreshing rest for the soul.

In all these adventures, God's spirit within—the topic of the next chapter—plays a great and often overlooked role. Jesus compared the kingdom of heaven to "treasure hidden in a field" (Mt 13:44). Let's see what we can find.

Questions and Invitations

- For Jesus to connect salvation with the faith of a little child implied an emphasis on the relation with God as our Father. What is it like for you to be childlike?

- How do you relate to the approaches to salvation listed here—childlike faith; being poor in spirit; asking, seeking, and knocking; and repentance?

- Living faith—receptive and active—is transformative. How much of the growth, power, and joy described in this chapter have you begun to experience? What would you like to experience more of? What can you do to enhance your progress in this area? Discussing with others will multiply your discoveries.

4
The Kingdom of God Within You

WHEN THE WORLD seems crazy and life feels hectic, there is a divine alternative—to live in a way that is increasingly centered in what countless persons have discovered. I often call it "the wonderfulness within"; this is an idea that is attractive to many people who do not believe in God. The reality of the spirit of God within each person is also the one of the most widely shared truths among the world's religions.[9] Interpretations differ, but they also overlap. In Jesus's concept of the kingdom of God, this is an essential teaching.

Jesus's concept of God as a Father implies a close, intimate relationship. The idea of God's spirit within is found in the Hebrew scriptures. "The spirit of man is the candle of the Lord, searching all the inward parts of his being" (Prv 20:27). God's spirit presence knows our thoughts and feelings, conscious and unconscious. Speaking on behalf of God, the prophet Ezekiel said, "A new heart I will give you, and a new spirit I will put within you" (Ezek 36:26).

Jesus compared the kingdom of God to treasure hidden in a field (Mt 13:44). His teaching of the kingdom of God within was a striking expansion of the popular concept of the kingdom (Lk 17:20–21). In the following sections of this chapter, we first examine the context of this teaching of Jesus. Then we consider the spirit within as revealing God as a unique Friend. This gift of God's presence plays a role in both kinds of spiritual experiences: those that are more ordinary, and those that are more memorable. Finally, we listen to the report of an unforgettable experience, shared by a student who recorded it as it unfolded in class.

Jesus Clarified Truths About the Spirit Within

In first-century Palestine, people were thinking of the kingdom of God mainly in terms of revolutionary historical change. It is understandable that some Pharisees tried to embarrass Jesus by asking him, "When is the kingdom of God coming?" Imagine their surprise when he replied, "The kingdom of God does not come with things that can be observed; nor will they say, 'Look, here it is!' or 'There it is!' For in fact, the kingdom of God is within you" (Lk 17:20–21).

The Pharisees asked about *when*, but Jesus knew what they truly needed: to realize *where* they could find it without having to wait. He could have said: "The kingdom is at hand now—see our group proclaiming the message among you. You can join." It would have been true to say this, but Jesus was pointing to something that cannot be observed. Spirit is not perceivable by the senses; nor is it a product of the mind. Spirit transcends both matter and mind. This is why most of the time we are not conscious of it and why so many people live as though it were not there.

It is noteworthy that these Pharisees did not have to be followers of Jesus to have the Father's spirit within them. Moreover, despite the fact that they had gotten seriously off the path, once the spirit had come, it stayed with them. I believe that God has taken up permanent residence in you during this life and the next, if you survive.

Jesus expressed the wonderfulness of the spirit within when he compared the kingdom of God to "treasure hidden in a field, which a man found and reburied; then in his joy he goes and sells all that he has and buys that field" (Mt 13:44). Selling everything symbolizes total commitment to finding the treasure again and again until we make it fully our own.

It is natural to ask how to find the treasure within. Jesus did not supply a roadmap; there are no instructions for conscious breathing or setting aside twenty minutes twice a day to close your eyes, take a few mindful breaths, and consent to the presence and activity of the spirit within. No single roadmap fits everyone's inward journey. Instead, Jesus told us *where* to look—within—and promised, "Search and you will find" (Mt 7:7). The invitation to seek can awaken curiosity and a spirit of adventure. Jesus's way of teaching leads receptive hearers into the arms of divine spirit.

The concept of the kingdom implies that God rules or reigns in humankind—to some extent now and eventually in heavenly fullness. God's reign is not an outward, military-political rule; rather, God becomes increasingly stronger in our hearts. To make the treasure of the kingdom within us truly our own, we must enjoy the presence of God's spirit in receptive faith; then active faith makes the decisions and carries out the courses of action that lead to growth. The influence of God's presence in our hearts becomes more dominant through the process of receiving love and goodness from our divine Parent—and then passing these blessings on to others. In doing this, we gradually become more God-like.

God as a Friend

In the ancient world, as now, it was important to have friends. The Hebrew Bible speaks of true friends in the Book of Ruth and disloyal friends in the Book of Job. The Book of Proverbs says, "A true friend sticks closer than one's sibling," and "He who loves purity of heart, and whose speech is gracious, will have the king as his friend" (Prv 18:24 NRSVUE, 22:11 RSV). We could say that this section is about having God as our number one friend in his kingdom.

Jesus often spoke of friends in his teachings and called people "friends" in a wide variety of situations. Here's a sample. The Son of Man was accused of being a friend of tax collectors and sinners (Mt 11:19). He spoke encouragingly to a crowd: "My friends, do not fear those who kill the body and after that can do nothing more" to harm you (Lk 12:4). And he will call us friends in a special sense of closeness if we do what he commands (Jn 13–15). When Jesus called someone "friend," he was expressing the truest love for, and faith in, the other person. Those who were receptive would have felt the blessing of the Master's friendship pouring into them.

If, as I believe, Jesus revealed God in his life and teachings, then his frequent use of the word "friend" makes it reasonable for us to regard the great and powerful Creator as our friend. We can develop friendship with God in large measure thanks to the spirit within, which helps us all to know God in our personal experience. But to find God—a process with no end in sight—the more sincerely, wholeheartedly, and persistently we seek, the more our search is rewarded.

The divine spirit within is a source of (among other things):

- Goodness and loyalty
- Energy and power
- Intuition and insight
- Joy and liberty
- Love and forgiveness
- Creativity and inspiration
- Peace and rest
- Meaning, purpose, and guidance in life

This loyal friend and constant companion is a great listener; it always supports us by encouraging the best in us. It is a wise counselor in every struggle, and also someone we can relax and enjoy with. Out of respect for our free will, this presence never interferes when unwanted and never forces anything upon us or manipulates us against our will.

At times, it is necessary for living faith to break through the barrier between the thickness of the human mind and the divinity of the spirit. But reaching for connection is mutual. It is like two teams tunneling through a mountain working from opposite sides and meeting in the middle—except that the spirit is on *our* side, cheering us on and helping us every step of the way.

If we desire to experience our Parent's love for us, we can turn to God's gift of the spirit, our personal "I love you." If we want to give this love to others, the inexhaustible Source is here. If we seek to know the will of God, it is not far off. If we want support in life's challenges, we have a friend whose attention is constant and whose power is never diminished.

If we consent and cooperate, the divine spirit can do much more for us, with us, and through us. In this way, *like the human Jesus, we are starting to reveal God.* When cooperation with God's spirit becomes an established part of our character, this achievement testifies to the crowning success of Jesus's message of the kingdom for an individual.

Two Kinds of Spiritual Experience

Some people think of spiritual experiences as unusual and impressive. I use the term more broadly. We don't need breakthrough insights or emotionally powerful religious experiences to become aware of the working of divine spirit. There is a beautiful kind of spiritual experience that fits its gentle uplift into the context of daily life. If we continue to develop our back-and-forth of interaction with divine spirit, this is all we need.

While we're discussing terminology, I would mention another term. I use the term "religion" with a minimal definition for my purposes in this book. By the term "religious," I simply mean that the experience puts one in closer touch with God; I should add, God or a functional equivalent, for example, Krishna in Hinduism or Amida Buddha in Buddhism. In my view, *a religious experience needs to be spiritual in order to be genuine; and a spiritual experience needs religious belief to be well understood.*

My world religions course would begin with Hinduism and its concept of the spirit within (the *atman*, which I "translate" as "eternal spirit self"). I would encourage the students to modify that concept however they wanted to in order to make it into something that they felt comfortable about putting into practice. Most of them chose centering prayer or conscious breathing to get in touch with their wonderfulness within.[10] After a few weeks some of them began to report experiencing new levels of calm, to take the most common example. I would say that *what I call spiritual experience can be explained in terms of neuroscience, social psychology, religion, or (my choice) all of these in varying degrees.*

There is a *continuous spectrum* from spiritual experiences that we hardly notice to ones that will continue radiating their influence for the rest of our life.

Garden-variety spiritual experiences

I use the term "garden-variety" to refer to common spiritual experiences that accomplish essential things. For example, we

- Sense that our prayer is putting us in touch with God
- Feel divinely loved
- Feel an inner emphasis being placed on a spiritual truth that we are reading or hearing
- Find our worship becoming more real
- Genuinely enjoy doing unselfish good for others
- Feel good about making a significant decision
- Know that we are not alone in working through life's struggles

Of course there are more types of examples. We respond to the question of how to discern genuine spiritual experiences as distinct from self-generated experiences in the section on discernment in chapter 7.

Taste-and-see spiritual experiences

When I speak of taste-and-see experiences, I am referring to spiritual experiences that are more vivid and memorable than garden-variety experiences. The distinction is a matter of degree, and the same phrases could refer to experiences in either category.

That being said, human beings have a God-given capacity to know divine spirit in a way that is akin to sense perception. Consider the psalmist's encouragement: "Taste and see that the Lord is good" (Ps 34:8). The psalmist is not only inviting us to experience divine goodness, but also to recognize God. The language of sensation is used because, in a very real sense, we can perceive divine spirit. God-knowing persons have a special consciousness of God.

The goodness of God is essential. There is an awareness that the greatest reality is good, loving, a source of happiness, personal, someone we can relate to, someone whose light outshines the things that we may find unwelcome to deal with, and a person who is in the business of transforming persons, the planet, and the universe in a grand process beyond our understanding. We can taste this experience, feel this love, grow as a result of this relationship, bring this greater reality into the rest of our lives, and find it in others, too.

In one way or another, this entire book is about seeing the whole of life as spiritual experience through the lens of Jesus and his gospel.

A Student's Taste-and-See Experience

We turn now to a high-energy spiritual experience. A student in a world religions class was writing during class, as I assumed, taking notes. I discovered later that she was writing a poem describing an experience that she was having in class. In her paper, she included the poem and introduced it this way:

> My concept for this paper is living as if the Kingdom of Heaven is within us, as Jesus preached. This concept builds on the concept of the universal family that we worked on last semester. It also deals with one of my main concerns about religion in the present time: the disconnect with God/the spirit that dwells within us. Hopefully, by living this way, I will gain not only a deeper insight into my own spiritual needs, but also a greater understanding of God.
>
> How does one go about living in this manner? Honestly, I am not sure, but I have my ideas. The groundwork was laid in the universal family project from last semester. Treating people as a sibling reflects the golden rule. However, this is not the only part of the Kingdom of Heaven. I believe the most important aspect, at least for me, is self-respect. You should have respect for the spirit/soul that dwells within the body. We should not berate ourselves for our wrongs, but ask for forgiveness. More important, we should not make ourselves feel inferior, because we deserve to be respected by ourselves, because of the spirit that we have. By no means does this mean that we should feel boastful or proud. Humility is very important to living the Kingdom of Heaven. Self-respect and humility

can live together harmoniously, but neither one can become extreme. It would throw off the balance of the spirit.

I do not know how this concept is going to work out. I had been struggling with a topic. Nothing had quite seemed to strike a chord in me. Then you assigned this paper, and I do not know if it was a time table or just the right time for a concept to come to mind. Unfortunately it did come right in the middle of class. I was afraid to close off the flood gate that had opened, so I wrote. I hope that you will forgive this indiscretion. I would appreciate any thoughts or suggestions that you have on this topic, or if you think it is worthwhile.

The light went on,
So bright.

It burned brightly,
For only a few minutes.

The light became too bright,
And burnt itself out.
The light bulb burst,
Sending glass shards everywhere.

My idea
That burnt so brightly,
Is gone.

Now I sit,
Trying to pick up the fragments,
And put my idea back together.

This student's humble sincerity, lofty project goal, and sustained seeking prepared her for this glorious taste-and-see experience. We can receive such gifts as revealing spirit realities and encouraging the faith of the individuals who receive them and others who learn of them.

The way that her experience ended was understandably troubling. In all gratitude to her gracious willingness to let me share this spontaneous writing, I would offer a thought that I could not come up with at the time. Something eternal has been revealed—to a maximum after which no more could be added that she could receive at the time. Hence, the "explosion." Fortunately, we retain such experiences in our memory, and they can continue to enrich us.

Summary and Transition

All kinds of people around the world have discovered a remarkable wonderfulness, often identified as the spirit of God within. Jesus said, "The kingdom of God is within you" (Lk 17:20). Jesus gave no instructions about how to find the kingdom within; on the inward journey of discovery, each person has a unique adventure in developing a closer friendship with the spirit. Largely due to the presence of this gift, we can know God as a friend. The spirit within plays a significant role in our spiritual experiences. Some of these are the ordinary "garden-variety" sort, including feeling good after worship or making a good decision or doing unselfish good for others. The more memorable experiences I call taste-and-see experiences, after Psalm 34, where we read, "Taste and see that the Lord is good." Our physical senses cannot perceive spirit or recognize God, but our deeper self, the soul, can do these things. This was illustrated in the student's experience report.

Growing up with Jesus, becoming centered in God, whose spirit lives within us, *we begin to live in a way that allows the spirit of God to live through us. This is how we reveal God.*

The life that Jesus lived was not a head-in-the-clouds pursuit of ever higher levels of extraordinary experience, nor a retreat from the challenges of his place and time. He was well-integrated and wisely balanced. For me, the wisdom of balance is illustrated by the countless young people who have gathered in retreats, sat around campfires, and joined in the song that begins, "This little light of mine, I'm going to let it shine." With smiles in their faces and love in their hearts, they express shared faith and commitment in an unselfconscious way, free of concerns about anyone's level of spiritual experience.

We transition now to build on how Jesus, beginning in childhood, balanced his life by becoming magnificently grounded in this world. He gained, and continued adding to, his excellent knowledge of nature and people on earth. He inspires us to integrate science with religion in daily life.

Questions and Invitations

- Have you discovered your wonderfulness within? How do you interpret it? What kinds of experiences do you associate with it? When you want to get in touch with it, what do you do?
- Imagine some things you could do for your mind to become a more hospitable place for the spirit of God within you to dwell.
- If you were to dedicate some time every day for a month or so to developing your friendship with the divine spirit—or with God—what would you do?
- What can you do right now to begin?

5

Jesus's Scientific Knowledge

MANY FACTORS HELP to shape us: our genes, our biological and social environment, early childhood experience, and the decisions of our free will. And after the liberation that comes with being born of the spirit, the effect of our decisions is greater. Intelligent and wise decisions can integrate our increasing awareness of spiritual and heavenly realities with our knowledge of material and earthly things.

This chapter grounds us in down-to-earth knowledge. We begin with some ideas about Jesus's early cognitive development and continue by setting forth the qualities that make him a pre-modern scientist. Then we consider some examples of his excellent knowledge touching on various fields: psychology, sociology, political science, history, and the interpretation of texts.

Finally, we consider, in Jesus and ourselves, how science can be applied in daily life. We begin to see how scientific living and spiritual living can go together.

Jesus's Early Cognitive Development

As children (and like so many animals), we experience a natural curiosity about the world around us. During the first year of life, we learn to see and hear things. Then we start developing language and cognitive abilities. For the rest of our lives, in the brain and the mind, these abilities are intertwined with our emotional and social life. For normal early childhood development, it is important to interact with dependable, caring adults and with other children. Empathy grows, along with the ability to consider a situation from another person's perspective; the golden rule is on the horizon. We enjoy play, games, humor, and the beginnings of artistic creativity. Then, as I see it, once we start to exercise our moral and spiritual capacities, we begin to actualize all of our basic human potential; we are now growing as whole persons.[11]

Thus, Jesus's knowledge of nature would have developed in the wider context of his life as a whole. I imagine him coming to know plants that were cultivated and in the wild; chickens, goats, sheep, and some wild animals; and desert and mountain wilderness.

As children, we explore and discover how things work. Even before we know the words "cause and effect," we are finding connections that make sense of the material world. We also learn about the social world, including our own reactions to it.

At first, our knowledge of things and people is mostly on the level of particular facts. This knowing comes from the experience of the inquisitive child, and it continues in adult life. We experience the satisfaction of inquiring and gaining intuitive insight, personally verifying and establishing with care some fact that matters. If it is controversial, it likely matters to us and to others as well. As we grow, our knowledge becomes more extensive, better organized, and more scientific.

Jesus, the Scientist

As the human Jesus grew, his faith in the Creator would likely have led him to realize that natural regularities—and what we call laws of nature—have a lot to do with the Creator's control of the natural world. In other words, the Creator makes science possible, invites us to discover his ways in nature, and generally rewards humans for gaining scientific knowledge if it is used for good.

We need knowledge to function effectively, to love people intelligently, and to serve them helpfully. Scientific knowledge enables us to know something of how the Creator has designed our universe.

The human Jesus might have had a variety of ways to acquire scientific knowledge. Four miles from Nazareth was Sepphoris, a provincial capital of the Roman empire and an urban center of Hellenistic culture. It was bustling with building projects that could have offered employment to Joseph and perhaps to Jesus as well. Sepphoris itself was on the major east-west caravan route, traveled by people from civilizations in the ancient world where sciences were beginning to emerge.[12] Someone who was interested in the world and its peoples could have learned all kinds of things from travelers who stopped nearby.

China had developed herbal medicine and a host of technological advances; and the road for trade connecting China with southwest Asia had opened. The Babylonians had compiled precise observations in astronomy. The Egyptians had made extraordinary achievements in architecture. The Greeks had begun mathematical physics and taken geometry and history to new heights. And the Romans had made strides in their technology and historiography.[13]

Assuming that Jesus acquired knowledge of carpentry from his father Joseph, he would have learned some geometry, properties of different kinds of wood, and all kinds of practical lore in using tools and maybe in dealing with various types of clients. He probably also sharpened his ability to think methodically and follow a sequence of steps to get a task done efficiently.

Whatever other knowledge Jesus acquired growing up, it is clear that he took great interest in people. His later teachings make it clear that he knew all kinds of people well. This is what makes his lessons so insightful.

Since the times of Jesus, science has advanced in many ways. But modern science grew out of premodern science. And all science develops from capacities of mind that the Creator has given us. Jesus showed some traits of a scientist. He was

- A keen observer
- Patient, not jumping to hasty conclusions
- Sharp in his reasoning
- Insightful regarding causes and consequences
- Able to express his insights in general terms
- Interested in a wide range of truths

Every person develops these qualities to some extent; Jesus attained excellence. We don't notice the scientist in Jesus because he expressed knowledge in vivid language accessible to everyone.

Examples of Jesus's Scientific Insights

Consider a few examples. I imagine Jesus as a young boy watching his father Joseph create a pile of sawdust when he would saw off parts of a big log to get a beam for a house. One day, he got a speck of sawdust in his eye, and a boy next to him tried to take out the speck in a clumsy way. Later in life he turned this into: "Why do you see the speck in your neighbor's eye but do not notice the log in your own eye? Or how can you say to your neighbor, 'Let me take the speck out of your eye,' while the log is in your own eye? . . . First take the log out of your own eye, and then you will see clearly to take the speck out of your neighbor's eye" (Mt 7:3–5).

The core of knowledge here is a general truth of psychology: "It is much easier . . . to identify and label the mistakes of others than to recognize our own."[14] See how Jesus used this truth. He did not talk like a teacher in a science class. Rather, he spoke with a vividness that would appeal to his hearers and help them remember. And he did so with a fresh touch of humor that softens the lesson and may intrigue us into thinking about what we are not seeing in ourselves that may be interfering with our attempt to do good to someone else.

Scientific realism and humor are both high priorities, and they are more powerful when artfully combined. When Jesus used animal metaphors to convey clear warnings, he expressed his insights with reassuring humor that could preempt the natural reaction of fear and anxiety.

A few examples. "Beware of false prophets, who come to you in sheep's clothing but inwardly are ravenous wolves." "Do not throw your pearls before swine, or they will trample them under foot and turn and maul you." "I am sending you out like sheep into the midst of wolves. So be wise as serpents and harmless as doves." Jesus's way with humor and images of (non-human) animals helps us not to dehumanize our opponents or enemies, who are still our siblings in the family of God. The animal images also suggest behavioral traits similar to some types of human temperament (Mt 7:15 and 7:6; 10:16 NKJV).

Jesus's humor also gives us a glimpse of our Creator Friend. If God has a sense of humor, dare we entertain the thought that the universe is ultimately friendly?

A sociological and political insight of Jesus touches on a central theme in this book: the importance of spiritual unity among believers. This teaching is a warning to families, cities, kingdoms, and other groups, including religious groups. "Every kingdom divided against itself is laid waste, and no city or house divided against itself will stand" (Mt 12:25). Here we have a general truth in sociology and political science with implications regarding the importance of spiritual unity in the kingdom of God. The warning to families stands in need of pondering today when the generation gap is often fraught with antagonism; at the very least, homes where parents are divided against each other tend not to provide the stability that children need.[15]

Jesus was also a master in another intellectual discipline, a science in the broad sense of the word. Hermeneutics is the discipline of interpreting the meaning of texts, for example, scriptures.

Jesus was called "rabbi" by people who appreciated his mastery of scripture. Jesus's understanding of the Hebrew Bible enabled him to teach in the Jerusalem Temple at age twelve and know which passage would best speak to particular circumstances, for example in his wilderness decisions after baptism.

But Jesus did not relate to people as a member of the intellectual elite. On one occasion he explicitly drew on his hermeneutical insight to refute a critic. This was in conversation with

Sadducees, who specialized in the first five books of the Bible and denied that the dead could be resurrected. They asked him a trick question about a man who died after he had been married to seven wives one after another: whose husband would he be in heaven? Jesus replied:

> "You are wrong because you know neither the scriptures nor the power of God. For in the resurrection people neither marry nor are given in marriage but are like angels of God in heaven. And as for the resurrection of the dead, have you not read what was said to you by God, 'I am the God of Abraham, the God of Isaac, and the God of Jacob'? He is God not of the dead but of the living." And when the crowds heard it, they were astounded at his teaching (Mt 22:23–33).

In his study of this passage, Jesus had recognized the implication of the tense of the verb—"I *am* the God of Abraham . . ." The present tense indicates a present relationship between God and the resurrected Abraham, Isaac, and Jacob.

Jesus's capacity to interpret scripture was based on hermeneutical disciplines, including excellent knowledge of the original language (Hebrew) and a close attention to the implications of grammar. In addition, his hermeneutical insight was also based on knowing God, and in particular, here, knowing the power of God.

Science and Religion in Partnership

We have seen something of the opportunities that the human Jesus had to learn about the sciences of his day from travelers near and far. From his father Joseph, he likely learned carpentry. Jesus acquired many strengths of a premodern scientist, and his insights embraced areas of knowledge that we could classify as psychology, sociology, political science, history, and hermeneutics.

We can also see how Jesus used his excellent knowledge. It was not only interesting for its own sake and for understanding more of the Creator's design; Jesus also used knowledge in his ministry to us. He would weave science together with vivid language that everyone could understand. And for dessert, he would add good humor, expressing relaxation and loving connection. This enabled some teachings that were challenging to be readily received.

Today the world needs to see spiritual values walking hand-in-hand with scientific responsibility. While some people look to science and technology to solve our major global problems, others look to religion. Jesus repeatedly brought forth a perspective that fully recognized both earthly and heavenly realities.

All our modern knowledge of causes and effects still leads back to the First Cause. The powerful, sovereign Creator has established the laws of nature, moral commandments, and the spiritual laws of love. To cooperate with these laws increases our practical effectiveness. Good knowledge, including good science, helps make our love intelligent.

Just a small step forward can be powerful. A student in one of my classes on science and religion took on an experiential project to quit smoking. He had tried before and failed. But this time he classified the temptations that arose as biological, psychological, or sociological. This simple use of science was enough, together with his motivation, to enable him to quit successfully.

We can always learn something more about health, psychology, pollution, and what we can do for our ecosystems. On divisive issues, we can reduce social antagonism and nurture empathy by seeking out high quality journalism and other kinds of knowledge, including what we can learn from others, whether they agree or disagree with us.

The habit of intelligently applying knowledge of the material realm and social domain is essential for excellence in daily life. I call it scientific living. The ideal of acting in the light of the truths of science is something we can experience in small steps. Select a simple task and take time to awaken your curiosity. Then bring to mind relevant truths of science that you already know and learn a little more. Then activate your spirit of adventure and go forth into action. In doing so, you can discover significant benefits from taking even a small step of putting scientific knowledge into practice.

In this way, we can experience for ourselves how *easy* scientific living can be, how *meaningful* it is to cooperate with the truths of the Creator's design, how *enjoyable* it is, and *how beautifully it complements spirituality*.[16] As we learn to understand the world, including ourselves, with greater care, and apply our growing knowledge responsibly, we contribute to progress in partnership with our Maker.

This inquiry is developed further in the next chapter. It focuses on righteousness and shows how scientific and spiritual living are united as we develop and exercise this virtue which meant so much to Jesus.

Questions and Invitations

- What personal growth project would help you become more like Jesus? List some of the facts about your growth need. What sciences are relevant to these facts? Bring to mind what you already know of science that is relevant to your project.

- Now learn a little more—from the most scientifically trustworthy sources that you have access to. What happens when you apply your knowledge as you begin to form new habits? Share your results with others, perhaps with vividness and humor.

6
Developing Righteous Character

SCIENTIFIC REALISM KEEPS our feet on the ground, reduces the risk of religious fanaticism, and bolsters sanity, which the planet needs more of. By contrast, spiritual idealism, living faith, energizes the child of God in growing up to be like our divine Parent. High ideals add meaning and purpose to life. Without goals, we muddle through, day by day, living largely on the level of biological needs, urges, struggles, and satisfactions. There is a dim sense that we are missing something. This chapter prepares us to integrate spiritual growth with progress in the rest of life; the result is holistic personal growth.

In first-century Judaism, a strong, balanced character centered in God could be described in one word: righteous. Righteousness was an umbrella virtue, including the other qualities of a good character. When Jesus was criticized for eating and drinking with sinners, he replied with a statement of his mission. "I have come not to call the righteous but sinners" (Mk 2:17, Lk 5:32). When Jesus referred to the righteous, he did not imply that these persons had never sinned in the sense of intentionally going against the will of God. But he did imply that they were neither lost souls nor rebels against God in grave spiritual danger.

I interpret Jesus's distinction between sinners and the righteous in a way that appeals to common sense and is also helpful in thinking about our ethical responsibilities. The righteous were sincere persons of faith who did a humanly decent job of following the commandments and living responsible lives in their communities. This involved personal moral standards and responsible habits in different spheres of life. These included trustworthy conduct in marriage and family life; honest dealing in commerce and restraint in the pursuit of wealth; consideration by political leaders for justice for all the people, not just the elites; and contributing in various ways to the religious community.

This idea of righteousness is not a humanly unreachable ideal of heavenly perfection, nor an extreme, fanatical legalism, but a quality of character that an ordinary person could acquire in this life.

Jesus's approach to stimulating the growth of righteous character was centered on transforming the inner life. He taught, "Seek first the kingdom of God and his righteousness." Here again, I highlight another beatitude which I regard as autobiographical. "*Happy are those who hunger and thirst for righteousness, for they shall be filled*" (Mt 6:33 and 5:6).

This chapter develops a concept of righteousness with four components. The first two portray how the human Jesus might have come to realize the happiness of this beatitude as a child. The last two, building on this beatitude, focus on this teaching: "*Be perfect as your heavenly Father is perfect*" (Mt 5:48). Although we can only attain the heavenly ideal after this life, the last component shows how to integrate the ideal with what we can all achieve in this life on earth. I finally share a student's experience report which illustrates some of the chapter's themes.

The Growth of a Righteous Character

Growing into the hunger and thirst for righteousness

I imagine that in early childhood Jesus sensed righteousness in his parents and in some of his neighbors. He naturally developed his God-given, human capacity for moral intuition of the difference between right and wrong. This intuition would have been shaped by his social environment, including passages from the Hebrew Bible.

In a family of love and laughter, play and wisdom, Jesus would have grown up in a well-ordered home. I cannot imagine his father Joseph imposing a rough patriarchy, laying down the law for everyone else. Wise discipline would have prevailed, including the just and fair resolution of disagreements. Some such arrangement would have helped Jesus feel secure growing up.

As Jesus came to know God, he would have increasingly experienced his heavenly Father's love. Naturally, he responded with love for God that grew to encompass all his heart, soul, mind, and strength. This total love for God would have motivated his *wholehearted desire to do God's will*. This level of desire I regard as *the heart of righteousness*. Wholehearted devotion to the will of God is equivalent to hunger and thirst for righteousness.

As these developments were going on in the inner life of Jesus, he would have realized that God is the perfection of righteousness. Then, I imagine, one day, reflecting on his experience of growth,

Jesus would have realized that he was becoming more like God. This would have made him very happy.

Realizing righteousness as a gift

In the second stage I imagine the young Jesus putting forth effort to become like God and discovering that his Father was increasingly fulfilling his great desire.

It is easy to imagine that, beginning sometime during his years in the local synagogue, Jesus cherished these words from Second Isaiah: *"My soul shall rejoice in the love of my God, for he has clothed me with the garments of salvation and has covered me with the robe of his righteousness"* (Is 61:10). The prophet implies that righteousness is not acquired by dutiful determination and grit. It is, above all, a gift. As the young Jesus pursued the ideals of the character of God, it is possible that he could have put forth effort and discovered that "God gives the growth" (1 Cor 3:7). Jesus was beginning the happy process of being filled with righteousness by his heavenly Father.

Jesus brought the present and the future into dynamic relationship when he taught that God will satisfy people who hunger and thirst for righteousness. He implied a connection between present happiness and the heavenly righteousness of our destiny. Although the complete fulfillment of the promise is beyond this life, there is no hurry. When faith and trust prevail, anxiety about being good enough is dissolved. Our long-term future is not in doubt. God-knowing persons have radiant assurance. In the matter of personal growth and other achievements, God gives the growth.

Taking up the quest for divine perfection

The hunger and thirst for righteousness unfolds into yearning to become and be like God. Jesus invited us into a magnificent destiny when he said, "Be perfect as your heavenly Father is perfect" (Mt 5:48). This command implies a promise: in partnership with God, we can achieve divine perfection.

To be perfect like God, who is spirit, is a perfection beyond anything we can attain in this life. This quest is completely fulfilled only in heaven. On earth, we can begin striving for the goal, and we can keep moving forward with God every day for as long as we live.

Today many people reject the very idea of perfection as a goal. They rightly reject unrealistic expectations that induce shame and guilt. Compulsive perfectionism about non-essentials can be part of the dynamic that generates self-righteous anger and contempt toward self and others.

By contrast, for Jesus, I believe, God's perfection of righteousness was based upon God's love and mercy—two of the most important qualities of God that we can live in a human way. What perfection meant for Jesus is expressed more fully in Greek: the word for perfect, *teleios*, also implies maturity and wholeness.

Jesus did not simply say, "Strive to become perfect." I believe that his present-tense imperative "*be* perfect" has implications for this life. If so, then there must be some kind of perfection, virtue, or mature wholeness that we can attain in this life on earth.

Integrating heavenly and earthly ideals with what is possible in this life

The human Jesus learned to live the will of God on earth as in heaven. We can, too. As we grow up to be like our Parent, we make decisions to do God's will of love by doing good to others. Ideally, this requires good knowledge of others and their situation, plus an awareness of the spiritual values that the situation calls for. But our practical goal is to be the best we can be day by day. This is where mustard seed growth comes in (Mt 13:31–32).

Jesus was continually expanding his knowledge of other people and the ever-changing circumstances of his time and place. And he attained an extraordinary awareness of divine values. His wisdom could often quickly connect his knowledge of relevant facts with the spiritual values that God wanted to actualize. Consider an example.

A person is driving on a highway and sees two cars on the side of the road that have evidently been involved in an accident. The driver sees the fact, intuits the cause, and spontaneously pulls over to help. The decision and action respond to the possible needs of those involved for values, including mechanical, medical, psychological, and spiritual. Drivers are not expected to have the scientific knowledge of a medic. But they might carry a small pack of first aid supplies in the car. Or carry or keep in the car a list of useful phone numbers. Or simply be a friend to someone who is shaken and in need of reassurance.

As we pick up tips and learn from experience and study about the material and spiritual dimensions of life, we automatically make adjustments, usually small ones, in our perspective, decisions, and actions. We combine scientific realism and spiritual idealism unconsciously.

The integrated virtue of righteous character has no definable threshold of how much scientific knowledge, spiritual realization, and philosophical wisdom are required. There are no flags waving at the finish line. But a certain habit of living begins to settle in. In every arena of our lives (home, school, work, and more), we make and carry out decisions that increasingly unite spiritual values with scientific facts. As long as our hunger and thirst for righteousness are alive, we will be blessed with ongoing growth.

Clearly, we need to use our intelligence to do the will of God. To mention this is controversial, since some people have more of it than others. But people can be liberated from seeing themselves in ways that demean the abilities that they truly have. And mercifully, *the spirit of God within each person is a cosmic genius.*

A Student's Living Faith in God's Gift of Righteousness

In my courses centered on experiential projects, I once assigned a project on righteousness in a world religions class. One student's experience report begins with an untitled poem describing an earlier struggle, which introduces the following selections from her paper.

> I was breaking down—shedding strength,
>
> * * *
>
> Caught inside of questions pulling from different directions,
> When the answer came in unexpected form:
> And it softly whispered: "Rest."
> . . . this single word was resonating with unmatched authority . . .
> So I said, "Yes. My soul welcomes this voice."
> Thus it continued:
> "Rest. This is not your time for searching.
> You are wounded, and your efforts are delaying the cure.
>
> * * *
>
> You are longing for answers, but needing so much more.
> Rest—and receive precious blessings from others;
> And through this you shall soon regain strength.
> Rest, tiny child,
> In the promise of my presence;
> And for *this* shall you learn to give thanks."

She confirmed having "fully and willingly received the *right* answer: 'find rest in the shadow of the Almighty,' for he is my God, and I trust in him" (Ps 91:1–2):

> I will no longer strain myself to accomplish what God will do in His own perfect timing. For this project, this means I will no longer strive for righteousness. I will not push the limits of my own abilities in an attempt to achieve a sense of morality equal to God's precise standard. Instead, I will observe the righteousness of my Lord. I will receive it from Him. I will soak it up. I will bask in its restorative power.
>
> The righteousness assignment's description invites us to begin "a fresh dimension of living." My life thus far has consisted of walking in circles—repeatedly crossing the same ground—making very little progress. But God promptly showed me a yet unvisited path which He wants my feet to follow, and it seems easy to say: "Yes, I will go." The beautiful objective is simply this: to seek the face of God.
>
> One might ask what it means to seek the face of God; and I'll admit I asked myself the same thing. How does one go about it? But if I choose to indulge this question, I would only be undermining my newest ambition to surrender all toilsome effort and labor to God. Not only this, but think what precious moments of potential experience might be lost because of an obsession over definition or method! That being said, my only answer for the person who *must* know what it means to seek the face of God is this: Let Him show you.

* * *

I felt God's face looking at me, and it felt warm. It felt like home. It felt like comfort.

Then, feeling guided to read Psalm 119, she found a new way of putting forth effort to work to attain ideals. "Without God's righteous authority, the world would be utter chaos. . . . How pleased the Father would be if we all understood the incredibly precious worth of his rules." Previously, she had thought that freedom meant "no dictates, no rules, no chains." Now she realized how the ways of obedience add up to "the greatest freedom: the experience of pure contentment."[17]

With wholehearted receptive and active faith, the author discovered her balance of patient trust and idealistic effort.

Summary and Transition

Nourished by high ideals, Jesus developed a righteous character. As I interpret it, when Jesus referred to "the righteous," he had in mind persons who are trustworthy in the various spheres of life: family, work, the political realm, and the religious community. To help his hearers grow in righteousness, Jesus's approach was to promote transformation of the inner life. A beatitude full of meaning to guide this process was, "Happy are those who hunger and thirst for righteousness, for they shall be filled" (Mt 5:6).

To envision the growth of a righteous character in Jesus and ourselves, I propose four components. First, receptive and active faith leads us to discover the goodness, mercy, love, and righteousness of God. Sincere beginnings grow into wholehearted cooperation with God, leading to important achievements. The key to human righteousness is the supreme desire to do the will of God. This desire is equivalent to the hunger and thirst for righteousness.

Second, as our righteous character develops, we discover that God is gradually making us like Godself. Each step of growth in our righteous character is a gift from God. Realizing this in our personal experience leads to happiness and rejoicing.

Third, an urge that was present in the first stage develops into the realization that we are in partnership with God on a wonderful quest for heavenly perfection.

Fourth, we develop the kind of perfection that we can attain in this life—the virtue of mature spiritual and ethical righteousness. We develop the habit of making wise decisions for the will of God by combining our increasing knowledge of situations with our growing awareness of spiritual values. As we continue to gain knowledge and spiritual insight, we often make appropriate adjustments in our lives unconsciously.

Finally, the student's experience report wrote about learning to balance exerting effort to obey divine commands and trusting God to give us righteousness on God's schedule.

When we speak of the will of God, the question arises of how we can find it, and this is the topic of the next chapter.

Questions and Invitations

- Are you a righteous family member, worker, citizen, and member of your religious community? Please select some areas in which you would like to get stronger.

- What factual honesty, what scientific realism, and what new learning could prepare you to make a good decision about what to do? What spiritual idealism, what higher meanings and values, what divine truth, beauty, and goodness, and what prayer are relevant to your decision?

- How can you integrate the realistic and spiritual dimensions into a wise decision?

7

Finding God's Will

THE VERSION THAT I learned of an old gospel hymn contains these verses.

> A blind man stood on the way and he cried (repeat); crying O, O, show me the way, a blind man, stood on the way and he cried.
> A preacher man stood on the way and he cried (repeat); crying O, O, show me the way, preacher man, stood on the way and he cried.
> Now *I'm* standin' on the way and I'm cryin'; (repeat) Crying O, O, show me the way, I'm standin', standin' on the way, and I'm crying.

Everyone has times when their soul is crying out something like this. When we are truly lost, we do well to express it sincerely and freely. The author of the Letter to the Hebrews writes: "In the days of his flesh, Jesus offered up prayers and supplications, with loud cries and tears, to the one who was able to save him from death, and he was heard because of his reverent submission" (Heb 5:7). In the hour of Jesus's agony in Gethsemane, when he needed assurance that the cross was indeed his Father's will, he was strengthened for the ordeal by an angel (Lk 3:9–46).

Jesus had doing God's will on his short list of essentials in the life of faith. He said, "Not everyone who says to me, 'Lord, Lord,' will enter the kingdom of heaven, but the one who does the will of my Father who is in heaven." Doing God's will makes us part of Jesus's new family. "Who are my mother and brothers? . . . Whoever does the will of God is my brother and sister and mother" (Mt 7:21 and 12:48–50).

If doing the will of God is so important, we can be assured from the start that God has a path that enables us to find his will. It must be a path so vast and universal that all persons of faith can find it, a path that contains within itself every other worthy path.

Sometimes we immediately and intuitively know the will of God; sometimes it takes searching before we get our intuition. And finding the will of God often involves a process in which we seek, find, discern, then decide and do God's will. This chapter reflects on Jesus's praying and on a parable. Then we clarify the problem of discernment, add a bit of philosophy, and solve the problem with three qualities of God—truth, beauty, and goodness.

When Jesus Prayed

Often the human Jesus did not need prayer in order to know the Father's will. As proposed in the previous chapter, fully mature righteous character—the kind of perfection that we can achieve in this life—integrates heavenly values with earthly realities. Jesus's intuitive insight into his Father's will was based upon his excellent knowledge of people and situations plus knowing God intimately, which often included awareness of the relevant divine value(s) to be actualized. For example, in the domain of truth, how much content communicated is enough? In the arena of beauty, would a parable or a direct teaching be more fitting? In the realm of goodness, does a situation call for patient waiting or courageous action?

But sometimes Jesus's wisdom was not enough to come promptly to an intuitive grasp of what to do. Then he would often have taken his longings and problems directly to God in prayer. I imagine an adolescent Jesus praying, opening himself in profound receptivity, allowing God to add to, and revise, his human wisdom.

A full prayer life includes quick prayers and long ones. Jesus probably prayed briefly and silently when no one else was aware of it. But from time to time, he would withdraw to a lonely place and pray. Sometimes he spent all night in prayer. He seems to have truly *enjoyed* communing with his Father for hours at a time. It is only logical that prayer to know God's will was part of Jesus's agenda in communing with his Father. After all, Jesus was energized by doing his Father's will. "My food is to do the will of him who sent me and to complete his work" (Lk 5:16, 6:12; Jn 4:34).

Prayer is different from seeking counsel from a human friend. Instead of a face-to-face conversation, it is a human mind and soul interacting with the spirit of God. Some people disregard the communication gap between humankind and God. They send forth lots of quick prayers and often assume that the next impressive input that enters their mind comes from God. Others are overwhelmed by the gap. They may be so anxious to be certain about God's answer that they agonize needlessly. Jesus lived and taught a better way.

The prayer that Jesus taught to the twelve apostles gives us the opportunity to enter into the prayer with Jesus in spirit and in truth (Mt 6:9–13). The prayer does much to orient us to God's will. We start by praying in the plural ("*our* Father"), which reminds us of our primary identity as children of God. Next, we are alerted to the fact that in prayer, we are on holy ("hallowed") ground.

Next: "Your kingdom come, your will be done, on earth as it is in heaven" (Mt 6:10 ESV). Entering into Jesus's prayer here implies that we are committing to accept and welcome whatever God does and whatever God does not do according to his all-wise will. In the same breath, the prayer calls us to do our part by doing God's will ourselves. The will of God is closely identified with the kingdom of heaven ("your kingdom come"). Not only does this concept imply eternal life for the family of those with faith in God and a wonderful destiny for our planet; we are also to do what we can here and now so that the will of God is increasingly done on earth as it is in heaven.

Then come requests for bread (material and spiritual), forgiveness, and help in dealing with evil. These petitions express a range of essential needs and suggest what we may be able to do to make God's love real for others. Here's the whole prayer.

> Our Father in heaven, hallowed be your name. Your kingdom come, your will be done, on earth as it is in heaven. Give us this day our daily bread, and forgive us our debts, as we also have forgiven our debtors. And lead us not into temptation, but deliver us from evil (Mt 6:9–13 ESV).

Jesus also experienced other modes of prayer, for example, chanting scriptures and other prayers that were a part of Jewish life.

Persistent Prayer

One of Jesus's parables may hint at the need for a more thorough prayer process:

> Suppose one of you has a friend, and you go to him at midnight and say to him, "Friend, lend me three loaves of bread, for a friend of mine has arrived, and I have nothing to set before him." And he answers from within, "Do not bother me; the door has already been locked, and my children are with me in bed; I cannot get up and give you anything." I tell you, even though he will not get up and give him anything out of friendship, at least because of his persistence he will get up and give him whatever he needs (Lk 11:5–8).

Persistence in prayer involves some combination of short and longer prayers. The one who comes knocking represents persistence; but persistence in prayer does not mean repeating the same demand over and over in an effort to get God—our friend!—to do what we want. Some people pray in order to change God's mind. But Jesus knew what the prophets knew about God. As Malachi said, speaking in the spirit, "I, the Lord, do not change" (Mal 3:6, 1 Sm 15:29).

When we sense that our prayer is not getting through, this may be our cue to try a new approach. Sometimes there is a need to find the prayer. In other words, we need to come closer to asking for what God knows we need.

The friend who did not want to get out of bed and help may have been stubborn. But we who have embraced the quest to become like our heavenly Parent can choose not to be stubborn about wanting the Creator to do what we want.

The friend who refuses to get out of bed may be said to be lazy. But we can choose to be diligent and do our homework before we pray—gaining understanding about the situation, the persons involved, and the relevant divine values. We also pray responsibly by not asking God to clean up our messes when we need to be held accountable by having to deal with the consequences ourselves (for example, ecological, social, economic, and political consequences). God does these responsible activities *with* us, not *for* us.

Before leaving the parable, let us savor the values of the friend who comes knocking. His request is unselfish; he is motivated by friendship and hospitality.

From the Problem of Discernment to a Solution

The problem

When we pray and expect an answer, things happen that some people interpret as divine hints, winks, or nudges. A-ha moments come, serendipities, and spiritual experiences; sometimes things happen which we interpret as acts of God, but they could equally be coincidences that were foreseen but not arranged by God. And sometimes, impressive inputs come from the subconscious mind.

An impressive response to prayer from the subconscious mind is more likely in quick prayers, but also possible in thorough praying. A quick prayer tends to be a prayer of the mind only, and not also a prayer of the soul. It may lack depth. But a quick prayer can also express such receptive, spiritual sincerity that it promptly receives God's answer.

Once we start working on a problem in the conscious mind, the unconscious mind may well go to work at the same time. It can draw on memories of quotations from scripture and other knowledge and experience of which we are not presently conscious. The mind may speak to us in the second person and give commands. An input generated by the human mind is not as wise as an answer from God, but it is often a significant improvement on what we had been consciously thinking previously.

The problem of discerning God's will is widely recognized. We hear the question, "How can we know God's will for sure?" The question has no simple answer. It can be asked in one way by a skeptic, in another way by an anxious believer, and in a third way by a trusting seeker. The skeptic doubts the possibility of knowing and uses this as an excuse not to seek. The anxious believer, faced by a complex moral question, may be seeking *intellectual* certainty that God may not provide. For a trusting seeker, prayer becomes an adventure of learning to cooperate with God. This adventure seeks the quality of certainty that satisfies the *soul*.

If we are uncertain and anxious, we can doubt our experience forever and raise endless questions about our efforts at discernment. This can paralyze decision-making, lead to skepticism, and cause us to lose our sense of humor. However, recognizing human limitations does not force us to be uncertain in our faith. If we persist, living faith finds divine assurance of progress on our journey in God.

Some resources for discernment are scripture, which must be translated, interpreted, and applied to the situation at hand; tradition, which is mixed; the judgment of the religious community or friends in faith, who can make mistakes; reason, which can be misused; and the test of time, which is not ideal either. The goal of fully consulting all of them is impossibly high, and not even in combination are they guaranteed to give us the divine answer. But they are worth taking seriously, because they afford a variety of perspectives and relax the tendency to overestimate our own judgment.

If there were a set of absolute criteria for determining the will of God, standards which the human intellect could apply without fail, there would be no adventure, no transformation, no soul growth, no stretching ourselves to live in a more heavenly way, and no fun.

When we struggle to find the will of God, it helps to recall that we already know a lot about it. For example, we can bring to mind the universal commands to love, to be merciful, to treat others as we want others to treat us, and to become perfect (to be our best, as we are able, one day at a time).

Next, the path to the solution to the problem of discernment leads through philosophy.

Philosophy's wisdom

Philosophy has an important role to play in sharpening our discernment. The word "philosopher" means "a friend of wisdom." The ideal is to live in the light of the wisdom we already have, to recognize when we need more, and then to seek for what we need until we find it. Philosophy can contribute to the larger process of seeking for God's will, because seeking, finding, discerning wisdom, and living wisely are also part of God's will.

In the Greco-Roman culture that would have stimulated Jesus's philosophical thinking, many thinkers sought to develop philosophy in a more comprehensive way. Some of them aspired to achieve an integrated understanding of reality and human experience. And the goal was to create a universal synthesis that would culminate in a philosophy of living.

In the ancient world and since, philosophical striving helped thinkers develop a variety of specific skills. At its best, philosophy replaces confusion with clarity, sharpens our capacities for intuition and insight, interprets meanings wisely, reasons logically, synthesizes concepts coherently, and knows when to be quiet because it would be unwise to say more.

In an informal and largely unconscious way, we each construct a philosophy of living as we grow up. We gather items for our wisdom basket from a wide variety of sources, including family, school, friends, and scientific, philosophical, and religious interpretations of reality. Wisdom also represents our harvest from seasoned experience, including lessons learned the hard way. This philosophy functions to organize the mind's grasp of meanings and values having to do, for example, with concepts of God, what it means to be a human being, and what kind of place the universe is (hostile, indifferent, or friendly). Our major concepts can be organized according to priorities that are centered in God and wisely balanced.

When we are unaware that we are functioning in a somewhat philosophical way, we may not see how important this activity is, and we are much less likely to seek out more education in this area. I regard modern civilization as seriously unbalanced, prizing science and material progress first, spirituality and holistic growth considerably less, and wisdom a distant third.

Some philosophers have noted that throughout the history of philosophy, we can find versions of three basic attitudes: dogmatism, skepticism, and adventuresome thinking. Dogmatism at its best is loyal to important principles, but it rejects balancing truths. Skepticism at its best sees important errors and criticizes incisively, but it does not know when to stop being negative. Adventuresome thinking is both oriented by basic truths and by learning from criticism.

Science, philosophy, and spirituality seek the kinds of truths that pertain to their own realm of matter, mind, or spirit. But all truth is God's truth, and philosophy finds meaning in all three domains. *Truth has a spiritual center, a scientific periphery, and a philosophical bridge between the two.*

It takes work to harmonize science and religion. For example, psychologist Sigmund Freud used his brilliant mind to criticize the concept of love for the neighbor. Consider a few of his criticisms, for example, about not becoming emotionally involved with everyone we meet, not trusting people blindly, and having psychologically healthy ways of dealing with our own aggression. We could foolishly say to ourselves that science has shown neighbor love to be a bad idea. Or we could transform these criticisms into warnings to make our love more intelligent and wise.

The following discussion of truth, beauty, and goodness is another example of philosophical interpretation. We cannot tell how much Jesus participated in the philosophy of his day; he probably did not organize his discernment as I do. Nevertheless, with a smile, I cannot help thinking that he must have agreed with some ideas that I regard as insightful.

Truth, beauty, and goodness in God's answer to prayer

Truth, beauty, and goodness are qualities of God and values that we can live. I regard them as divine values because we find them on all levels. In God, in the mind, and in the material world, we can discover truth, find and create beauty, and participate in doing what is good. These universal values enable the Creator Parent and the creature child to share a common language.

I see truth, beauty, and goodness as a ladder that God puts down from heaven to earth so that there is something we can understand that enables us to climb higher. These values speak to our thinking, feeling, and doing. If a seeming answer to prayer feels good, but is intellectually problematic, or appeals intellectually but doesn't feel right, or can't be put into practice, then we can wrestle with it more or simply reject it.

God is the source of these three values; and "God is love" (1 Jn 4:8). I regard these values as forming a path to love and as being essential ingredients in love. The highest truths are truths of love, and love is the most fulfilling beauty and the greatest good.

Truth, beauty, and goodness prepare us for all manner of situations in which we must decide and do. God does not call on the phone or materialize a print-out or a roadmap. But faith receives guidance that is sufficient to clarify our choice. Then the decision launches the doing—the course of action.

As God responds to our prayer, the Creator does not put the three values on a plate like a pineapple, a banana, and a mango. Instead, God gives a blend, a smoothie, that we can find delicious without having to ask about these three values.

I find that a response to prayer that blends truth, beauty, and goodness can include:

- Clear intuition or insight into the *truth* of the situation being prayed about

- Moral insight into the *goodness* of the course of action that opens up

- An intuitive feeling, peaceful or rejoicing, in response to the *beauty* of seeing these values come together

In such insights and intuitions, we discern God's values.

Amazingly, these same qualities of clarity (truth), moral satisfaction (goodness), and peace (beauty) can come after quick prayers.

Why then should we take time to explore truth, beauty, and goodness? For the same reason that Jesus prayed to the Father at length. It might seem that he could have contented himself with quick prayers. But longer periods of time in prayer cultivate the mind in such a way that our quick prayers are more likely to come closer to what God wants us to find. Otherwise, quick prayers might seem a little bit like a game.

In the game of darts, players take turns trying to throw their darts so that they stick in the center of the dartboard. But most of the time they hit the dartboard somewhere else; sometimes they miss the dartboard altogether. If I were going to create a dartboard, the center would symbolize doing God's will, and the surrounding circles would represent human approximations to that goal that are less divine.

Here is the solution that I propose to the problem of discerning the will of God. Because divine values are woven together in religious experience, we ideally need to reflect in order to distinguish them in a response to prayer. Our thinking finds truth in it; our feeling finds beauty in it; and we find goodness in its guidance for our decision. When we have been wholehearted in our prayer process (even a quick one when that's what we have time for), we may rest content with the best that we have been realistically able to find.

In loving mercy, God works with us to help make the best of our decision. The Parent accepts and adopts the child's best effort. We can relax and rejoice. *Discernment doesn't have to hit the bullseye; it just has to hit the target.*

Discernment does not mean intuiting whether the source of an impressive input is human or divine. Discernment means intuiting truth, beauty, and goodness.

It is our choice to explore this frontier. The more we try it out, the more interesting it becomes.

Summary and Transition

Sometimes we know the will of God intuitively. At times we do well to cry out, "Show me the way." This chapter has unfolded an adventuresome path of mobilizing our human powers to cooperate with God in seeking and discerning his will.

We speculated on Jesus's practice of quick prayer and gave evidence of his persistent prayer. We considered a parable that may suggest a more thorough prayer process. Next, after we seem to have received a response to our prayer, a question may arise about whether the input comes from God or from the human mind. Facing the problem of discernment, we looked briefly at some resources, and at philosophy in particular.

I then set forth the proposal that a divine answer to prayer brings truth for thinking to understand, beauty for the heart to feel, and goodness to govern our doing. All these values are woven together, so we may need to reflect on our experience to detect them. But having been wholehearted and persistent in our prayer process, if we are to avoid skepticism (giving up on the effort of discernment), we have every right to go forward trusting that the will of God (our friend) is to adopt and work with the best we can find. If we have not hit the bullseye, we have indeed hit the realistic target, which is all that our Parent asks of us.

Sometimes I think of God's will in terms of *that, what,* and *how*: God's will is *that* we wholeheartedly desire to do it, to discern *what* he wills, and then to find *how* to do it in a loving and merciful way. Being wholehearted about God's will makes the *what* and the *how* much easier. Note that, after we have found God's will, it is sometimes better to live it unconsciously. For example, with the golden rule, self-conscious rule-following is not the highest level; loving spontaneity is best.

After discernment, what comes next is to actualize God's will, to make it real, by deciding and doing. On the basis of the introductory chapters, we are now in a position to appreciate Jesus in action at age twelve. In the next chapter we see him in the Temple in a way that shows his developing character and expands our concept of what it means to be well-balanced.

Questions and Invitations

- When you want divine guidance, how much do you rely on quick prayers?

- What sources of wisdom do you rely on most?

- When you pray longer, what do you do? After reading this chapter, is there anything that you would like to add to what you do?

- Jot down some notes that describe an experience of answered prayer. In your description, include what truth, beauty, and goodness you find to be present in that answer.

8

Jesus at Age Twelve

JESUS WAS BORN in Bethlehem; but not long after, he was taken to Egypt for his safety, because the paranoid and violent King Herod had sent out soldiers to kill him. After Herod's death in 4 BCE, Jesus and his parents moved to Nazareth in Galilee, where the child spent most of his early years (Mt 2). Jesus's growth before age twelve was summarized by Luke: "The child grew and became strong, filled with wisdom, and the favor of God was upon him" (Lk 2:40). These phrases indicate the goals that I repeatedly propose for growing up with Jesus: to develop a strong character, wisely balanced, and centered in God.

It is at age twelve that we see Jesus in action for the first time. An important pair of events reveals the kind of person that he was becoming. They took place in the Temple in Jerusalem, where he went with his parents and many others from Galilee for the annual Passover feast, which celebrated Moses's leading his people out of Egypt into freedom.

We can trace their probable route from Nazareth to Jerusalem. The village of Nazareth was fifteen miles west of the southern tip of the Sea of Galilee, and sixty-five miles north of Jerusalem. Immediately to the south of southern Galilee was unfriendly Samaria, so the travelers from Nazareth would likely have gone mostly east around Samaria, then south on the east side of the Jordan River through friendly Perea, until they were close to Jericho, which was on the road to Jerusalem. It would normally have taken five to seven days for the group walking together from Nazareth to cover the journey of over ninety miles.[18]

Jesus Taught in the Temple

At the Temple, Jesus likely went through his coming-of-age ceremony, something like a bar mitzvah, to become a "son of the commandment." If so, he was now regarded as responsible for his own actions. He was a full member in the Jewish community, one who could read scripture in the synagogue, conduct services, and participate in the Temple discussions.

Intentionally or not, Jesus got separated from his parents after their stay in Jerusalem, when they set off with the crowd returning to Galilee. However it happened, he realized that God had a purpose for him; and he made the decision to stay behind to take part in these Temple discussions.

Jerusalem hosted the headquarters of a world religion. For the most important holy days, Jews came there from Europe, Africa, and Asia as well as what we call the Middle East to pray and worship, pay the Temple tax, and arrange for sacrifices. The seventy-one members of the Sanhedrin functioned as a supreme court of religious law, meeting almost daily.[19] At the Temple, learned teachers would discuss and debate.

Into this distinguished group came a twelve-year-old from Nazareth. He sat "among the teachers, listening to them and asking them questions. And all who heard him were amazed with his understanding and his answers" (Lk 2:40–52). These two statements suggest a lot. Jesus was functioning like a rabbi, a trained teacher. We can infer that during his years in his local synagogue, he must have been an outstanding student of the Hebrew Bible. To gain the support he did in the Temple discussions, his way of teaching must have been respectful and fair, free of antagonism. Jesus was teaching then, as he would often do later, by asking questions. And they asked him questions, too. The report gives the impression of an open, interactive style of teaching.

The Interruption and Jesus's Balanced Response

For the first full day of their trip with the crowd returning to Galilee, Joseph and Mary did not realize that their son was not with them. After returning to Jerusalem, they spent three days looking for him. When they found him in the Temple, Jesus was completely caught up in the discussion.

During this high point in his life, interacting with the leadership of Israel, Jesus heard his mother break in. "Child, why are you treating us like this? Look, your father and I have been anxiously looking for you."

It is natural that parents who had lost a child for three days would be distraught. But she interrupted the entire proceeding, and addressed Jesus with a term, "child," that did not fit his new status and manner of functioning.

When surprised by her, Jesus responded by asking two questions: "Why were you searching for me? Did you not know that I must be about my Father's business?" (Lk 2:49 NKJV).

On the one hand, we see here Jesus's strength of character, centered in God. He had acquired a definite sense of his mission as a teacher. His defense of his staying in Jerusalem for the Temple discussions implied that one's first duty is to do the will of God. We have reason to believe that Jesus's questions to his parents were free of defiant, defensive-aggressive challenge.

Reading words on the page hardly conveys what it would have been like to see and hear Jesus. I once participated in a workshop led by an actor and theater director who assigned pairs of us to read aloud stories of brief interactions between individuals and Jesus. It was fascinating to have to decide *how* to say what Jesus said. All of a sudden, we had to stop and think. He communicated not only ideas in words that can be written down; he also communicated attitudes and feelings. Reading silently, we normally do not ask ourselves about such things. But if we understood Aramaic, the language in which he taught, and could watch a movie of Jesus, hear his voice, and see his gestures, we would recognize how incomplete our reading is. We unconsciously make assumptions about the feeling dimension of the story.

After raising his two questions, Jesus gave the second part of his response to his parents: in silence, he left the Temple with them, beginning the journey back to Nazareth. His departure showed his ability to coordinate his first duty to God with obligations to other persons.

I imagine that he walked out, not looking down at the ground in humiliation, nor angry and resentful, but with dignity, his head held high, and with compassion and respect for his beloved parents. After all, God's will includes human obligations, too, for example, to "Honor your father and your mother" (Ex 20:12). I find a beautiful balance in this twofold response.

When I speak of balance, I do not imply that every value has equal weight. True balance in life is only achieved when we put God first, and God's righteous character is always balanced. What we see in Jesus's response is true for us, too. Strength without gentleness is brutality; gentleness without strength is weakness.

How Family Life May Have Prepared Jesus's Balanced Response

By age twelve, Jesus would have strengthened his character by working through the disagreements that normally arise between children and their parents. The child does something that goes against the parent's expectations. Or the parent says something, and the child disagrees. The convictions of an intelligent and vigorous child could not be expected to agree with every traditional idea, practice, and expectation of the parents.

When differences like this arise, what options does a child have? Immaturity sees only two: suppress one's own convictions, or rebel. In the Temple episode, the first thing that Jesus did was to affirm that what he was doing was his Father's will. So it is clear that Jesus had not chosen a strategy of passive submission to his parents. Next, he obediently left the Temple with them. This shows that he did not allow his own views to develop into rebellious self-assertion, doing whatever he wanted in spite of family obligations.

Avoiding immature extremes, Jesus found a mature third way. He seems to have learned to listen to his parents, to respect them, and to be fair regarding what they asked of him. Jesus would also have discovered that, when disagreements arise, sometimes a good compromise is possible, sometimes not. And sometimes his parents made decisions that he simply had to put up with. In the first case, we develop the virtue of teamwork; in the second case, cooperation needs extra stamina to sustain good will in making the best of the decision that has been made.

If this idea about Jesus's balance of character is correct, then his love for his parents would have acquired a maturity that cannot be had by any spiritual shortcut. The will of God does not take us away from earthly responsibilities; on the contrary, it leads us to develop a balance of virtues that help us coordinate our duty to God with our social obligations.

The virtues that Jesus gained by working through such difficulties at home are transferable. They apply at work and elsewhere. Learning to listen well and respect people regardless of their views, and the ability to work together as part of the majority or the minority—these qualities make for enduring, harmonious, and effective organizations. I would think they apply in any civilization.

Luke summarizes the time between Jesus at age twelve and his baptism by stating, "Jesus increased in wisdom and in stature and in divine and human favor" (Lk 2:52).

Conclusions, Projections of Further Growth, and Transition

Now we can see more of the value of experience in the human family, God's 'plan A' for our growth. There is evidence to support the idea that basic strengths are ideally learned in the family.[20] We glimpse the possibility that working through tensions that arise in daily life leads to acquiring more virtues that strengthen the family bond. These qualities include, on the one hand, the courage to speak up for one's own convictions and, on the other hand, the ability to hear, understand, and openly and fairly express appreciation for others' views. In addition, there is the will to act constructively whether or not a good compromise is possible. Every virtue gained contributes to the quality of our love. In this way, the human family prepares us for life in God's worldwide family.

When we focus too narrowly on daily struggles, we easily lose sight of the cosmic perspective: going through trials is part of the Creator's design for our growth. Jesus did not grumble in the face of difficulties. He seems to have taken them on with a positive attitude as part of living the will of God, whom he loved so much.

Consider the facets of growth that we have already reviewed, and imagine the progress of the human Jesus continuing to the time of his baptism. His receptive faith would have deepened to fullness, and his active faith gained excellence in a wider range of tasks. His relationship with the spirit of God within him grew closer than we can imagine. His understanding of Jewish tradition was superior to that of the experts. His knowledge of the world would have further developed his scientific realism to balance his growing awareness of divine truth, beauty, and goodness. His righteous devotion to the will of God would have brought his quest for perfection to the heights of human potential. He would have attained a level in discerning the Father's will of often "hitting the bullseye." Now he was ready to deploy in his public career a superbly strong character, wisely balanced, and centered in God.

Having pondered decisions that Jesus made at age twelve, we have a better vantage point for reflecting on the far-reaching decisions that he made surrounding his baptism, the topic of the next chapter.

Questions and Invitations

- Have you learned to balance strength and gentleness?

- Do you ask good questions?

- Do you integrate your discernment of the will of God with human obligations?

- What implications regarding family life does this chapter have for you?

9

The Decisions That Launched Jesus's Public Ministry

HAVING SKETCHED THE growth of Jesus during his early years, we now see him in his late twenties or early thirties. He has, I believe, achieved the height of the human potential for growth. He is fully ready to make the powerful decisions that will launch his public ministry. Much was at stake in coming to John's baptism and then afterward in the wilderness.

To Fulfill All Righteousness

It may seem obvious that Jesus would go to be baptized in the Jordan River by his relative and forerunner, John (Mt 3). I do not imagine that Jesus debated it in his mind, but I do believe that he thought deeply about its implications, communed with his Father, and made a full, deliberate, conscious choice to do the divine will.

John proclaimed repentance as the way to prepare for the coming of the kingdom of God. When Jesus was about to be baptized, John protested: "I need to be baptized by you . . . do you come to me?" John's question implies that the baptizer is normally greater than the one who is baptized.

In reply, Jesus stated a deeper reason for coming to John: "to fulfill all righteousness" (Mt 3:15). In doing so, Jesus openly connected the beginning of his public career with the work of his forerunner, whom he would call greatest—perhaps partly because he was the prophet who recognized Jesus and would proclaim the Master for who he was (Mt 11:11). The wider meaning of this baptism was that it marked the beginning of the most momentous years in Jesus's life. God had made a covenant with Abraham: Moses, Elijah, and the prophets had led the way forward. It was the will of God that Jesus's followers should nourish themselves on the best of this heritage. Moreover, his coming for baptism confirmed John's message about preparing for the coming kingdom of God; John could go forward in confidence and prepare his followers for the new teacher who would baptize them with the Holy Spirit (Mk 1:8, Acts 1:5).

The Risks Connected with God's 'Plan A'

By the time Jesus came on the scene, Judaism had been divinely sustained since the time of the covenant two thousand years earlier. The network of synagogues, centered on Jerusalem, was extensive. For this network to carry Jesus's message would have been the ideal first step in the gospel becoming established worldwide. It seems plausible to regard this as God's 'plan A.'

But in addition to being loyal to his Father's will, Jesus was also realistic. Knowing the mindset of the religious leaders, he would have recognized the possibility that they would reject his mission. Jesus could conceivably have gone somewhere else and started a new religion free of the language of kingdom and Messiah, with their misleading and dangerous political and military connotations. But Jesus went to John for baptism in order to embrace 'plan A.' This required him to fulfill all righteousness by completely dedicating his will to the doing of his Father's will.

In response, in the voice at the baptism, God said: "This is my beloved Son, in whom I am well pleased" (Mt 3:17 NKJV). I believe that God's pleasure in his Son indicates Jesus's achievement of human perfection. This part of his mission was fulfilled.

The Wineskins Problem

Lucid about the difficulties he faced, Jesus said that one doesn't "put new wine into old wineskins" (Mt 9:17). This metaphor is based on the fact that when new wine ferments in old wineskins, it produces carbon dioxide. The gas expands and causes the wineskins to break and the wine to spill out. This image symbolized the fact that the religion of Jesus, the religion of the spirit, could not be made to fit into a rigid framework. The hope was for a critical mass of religious leaders to become flexible enough to accept the new message and allow their tradition to be renewed. Jesus would try his best to win over these people. To fulfill all righteousness meant embracing the difficulties and dangers of the divine way with its ups and downs and its long-term progress that mostly goes slowly.

The wineskins problem has repeatedly caused division; this occurred among the followers of Jesus not long after he left the planet, and it is still with us today. One group remains loyal to what it regards as the truth of tradition, while another group advances what they regard as the new truth that is needed now. The problem is to distinguish between what is enduringly true in one's religious heritage and what is inflexible wineskin that needs to be replaced by something better. One also needs to discern the difference between timely truths and popular errors.

Jesus's response to this problem is a model for us.

- The Master was neither a one-sided traditionalist nor a one-sided innovator. He upheld eternal truth that had been voiced in the past, even as he proclaimed new truth to liberate his hearers.

- From the beginning, his approach was positive. He did not expose and attack the errors of tradition until extreme circumstances and God's timing indicated that he should change his approach (chapters 17 and 18).

- He emphasized truths held in common, sometimes quoting selected images and insights from scripture.

Understanding the structure of the wineskins problem and knowing Jesus's strategy, we have guidance for our efforts in sharing his teachings today.

Confronting Rebellion Against God

After his baptism, the Son of Man went alone into the wilderness for forty days. There he encountered and triumphed over three temptations that were relevant to his public ministry. His decisions in response to these temptations would guide the outworking of the commitment to all righteousness he had just made by coming to John for baptism.

To understand the three choices of Jesus, we need some background. God and human beings are not the only personalities who inhabit the universe. There are other beings, too, higher than humans and lower than God; and they, too, have free will. Many thousands of years ago, a high being started a rebellion against God. "War broke out in heaven" (Rv 12:7). The devil came to this world to bring sin—deliberate rebellion against the will of God.

It was the devil that did the tempting. Jesus did not experience temptation in the ordinary sense of the word. His replies were immediate and strong. He never wavered, never entertained the possibility of compromise, was never torn in his soul and needing to pray. He did not need to deliberate about facts and values. In each case, the choice was whether to gain a secondary value at the expense of God's way. Jesus knew exactly what was at stake, and he was fully aware of God's will. He judged intuitively and insightfully; his responses were far-seeing and decisive.

Jesus's Three Wilderness Decisions

Jesus's three decisions cover the material, intellectual, and spiritual dimensions of life (Mt 4:1–11). To each of the devil's proposals, Jesus responded simply as a righteous human being, strong in the power of faith, well-provisioned with truth, and secure in God. To each temptation, he replied by citing a passage from the Hebrew Bible. He thereby implied that ordinary, God-knowing, human beings can triumph over any temptation whatsoever.

The first temptation had to do with satisfying normal, natural, material needs. Human beings are very material creatures. The

Creator has placed us at the beginning of our journey to heaven in this amazingly designed body, with its needs and desires, pleasures and pains. But these can become chains that bind. The Creator provides for needs to be met and pleasures enjoyed; however, sometimes one must choose between gratifying self and pleasing God.

When Jesus was hungry, the devil said, "Command these stones to become loaves of bread." Jesus replied: "Man shall not live by bread alone, but by every word that comes from the mouth of God" (Dt 8:3). His response implied that he would satisfy his material needs in ordinary ways, like other human beings do. With Jesus, we pray, "Give us this day our daily bread" (Mt 6:11). We acknowledge the Creator as the source and ultimate provider for human needs. We pray in the plural, knowing that the Creator does not want any of his children to starve. But if food comes at the price of a bargain with the devil, it is better to go hungry.

The second temptation had to do with how to pursue idealistic goals. Some people use all their talent, skill, money, and power to pursue success with sensational and forceful means. But in spiritual work, the methods we use must fit the God we serve.

The devil tempted Jesus to throw himself off the top of the Temple, trusting the angels to keep him from falling. Had he done so, the impact on the crowds would have been sensational. What a way to win followers! But what kind of followers would they be? Their enthusiasm for miraculous signs and wonders would upstage the message. Jesus replied: "Do not put the Lord your God to the test" (Mt 4:7, Dt 6:16). True persons of faith don't play games with God; they don't do unwise things assuming that divine providence will intervene to save the day. This decision implies that Jesus's healings and other wonders were not done to dazzle people into believing in him. In most cases, they were done in response to others' faith.

The third trial was about whom we worship and what we most want. The devil offered to give Jesus the kingdoms of this world, if the Master would only agree to worship him. If Jesus had used his human and superhuman powers to lead an army against Rome, he would surely have been heralded by the Temple leaders and the people as the Messiah.

But anything that might have been gained by departing from God's way was nothing compared to Jesus's highest commitment: "Worship the Lord your God, and serve only him" (Dt 6:13). To worship and serve only God means that we serve others only in accord with God's will.

In this challenging interaction, the human Jesus endured a visit from the personification of lies, ugliness, and sin—and emerged victorious. Another part of his mission, perhaps. Indeed, Jesus showed how we can handle temptation. It should be noted that when we experience temptation, we should not conclude that the devil is present. The human heart can generate plenty of temptations on its own. Said Jesus, "From out of the heart of man, come evil thoughts, sexual immorality, theft, murder, adultery, coveting, wickedness, deceit, sensuality, envy, slander, pride, foolishness" (Mt 15:19, Mk 7:21–22).

This frank statement about evil that can come out of the human heart helps us understand ourselves and others realistically. When we are living at our best, these potentials are dormant. But when they are stirred up, we do well to take them seriously by going first to God or Jesus, and perhaps getting help from a friend or a counselor.

I believe that full maturity for everyone includes major decisions that cover self-mastery on the material level, the righteous use of our powers, and a supreme commitment to God.

The Way of Life Versus Evil and Sin

In order for Jesus to reveal the heavenly way of life on earth, he seems to have needed to confront the opposition. To understand what Jesus overcame, we need to make a distinction between evil and sin. The Creator's plan of biological evolution brought forth humankind with natural tendencies toward material-mindedness and self-centeredness. The *potential* for evil is unavoidable. But we can choose good instead, when we are old enough to know the difference.

When we get tangled up in evil, our own, others', or both, we can enter into Jesus's prayer, "Deliver us from evil" (Mt 6:13). When this prayer is full of faith, God's answer empowers us to live the values of the divine way.

Sin is in a different league. Sin rejects morality, betrays divine values, and rebels against the will of God with eyes wide open. Sin is not the archer who misses the mark, but the one who defies the very idea of a target and shoots arrows at other archers. Sin knows what God wants but has stopped caring or takes pride in defiant action.

The way of life stands in contrast with evil and sin in many ways.

- The way of life says 'YES' to God and goes forward. Evil is self-deceived; it goes the wrong way but does not allow itself to face honestly what it is doing. It may mistake its own vice for a virtue and cause atrocities. Sin is proud of living in reverse.

- The way of life uses free will to seek and do what is good. Evil pursues satisfactions that are wrapped up in self. Sin asserts the deceptive freedom of doing whatever one feels like and ends up with bitter consequences.

- The way of life faces problems with effective focus, a merry heart, and tenacious resilience. Evil procrastinates and takes the easy way out. Sin gathers its forces to distort truth and love.

- The way of life aspires to love each person appropriately. Evil gives affection only to those who are affectionate in return. Sin finds allies only in the company of those who pridefully blind themselves to God's goodness and the privilege of serving our siblings.

- The way of life leads to a glorious future. Evil slows down progress for everyone affected. Sin can accumulate momentum that strangles a person's destiny as a child of God. In other words, if sin becomes a hardened habit, the individual becomes increasingly deaf to any further merciful appeal. In the worst-case scenario, "the wages of sin is death"; in other words, the final consequence is a death which amounts to spiritual suicide of the soul (Rom 6:23). This is not to be confused with the desperate overdose of a teenager seized by the illusory darkness of depression.

From God's all-knowing perspective, one's life between birth and death shows where one's center of gravity is—on one side or the other of the great divide between the way of life and the way of death. True, our growth is incomplete; we wander and stumble. Only God knows the heart, only God can judge. In mercy and patience, he forgives again and again. But God knows when he is being consciously and deliberately rejected, and he knows when that rejection amounts to an individual's final answer.

Jesus wept over Jerusalem as he anticipated the consequences of the sin that was brewing in the Sanhedrin, the ruling group who met in the Temple (Lk 19:41). I imagine Jesus weeping over our sins as they violate the Creator's wise laws, weaken character, damage our connection with God, harm others, and make it harder for the planet to realize its destiny.

Who has not fallen into evil and sin? But the good news is that transforming, divine forgiveness is ours to accept.

Jesus's personal triumph over even super-human tendencies to evil and sin was complete by the time he had concluded his wilderness decisions. When Jesus said, "Which of you convicts me of sin?" he implied that he had never sinned (Jn 8:46). His character had acquired the strength that came from the momentum of consistently living the way of life for decades. Growing up, he gained a balance of virtues derived from experiencing a range of challenges. And his character was centered in the righteous will of the God of love and mercy.

Seeking the maturity of Jesus is like a pilot in an airplane—more or less continually buffeted by wind currents to go up or down, left or right. These currents may not be strong, but they require the pilot to make course corrections in order to stay on track toward the destination. Ideally, a well-balanced character remains steady no matter what direction the next push or pull comes from.

Summary

To look back on this chapter, we have considered four challenges that Jesus faced in launching his public mission. In each, he responded with a decision that fulfilled all righteousness. He chose to:

- Wholeheartedly accept his Father's will for his public career as a teacher even though he knew that the wineskins of tradition might be unable to receive the wine of the religion of the spirit

- Exercise self-mastery over the needs and desires of the body
- Commit to using his powers only in ways that were consistent with the spiritual character of his mission
- Decide wholeheartedly to worship God alone and serve only him rather than to pursue the political aims of a false Messiah

Jesus acquired righteous momentum by making the countless decisions day by day that established the habits of action that helped to form his character and laid the foundation for his magnificent performances leading up to and following his baptism by John.

I would add that an insightful, breakthrough decision does not take me very far. To form good habits, I have to repeat my best decisions again and again in order to make them trustworthy. A decision can fall asleep on me and may need new life breathed into it. I find that there is great power in converting a noble but tired decision into an authentic and wholehearted moral and spiritual decision.

The last three sections—on the devil, the wilderness decisions, and the human temptations to evil and sin—include many examples of what a God-knowing person desires to be free of. We have read a long list of evils, considered the extremes of sinful rebellion against God, and pondered the contrasts of evil, sin, and the way of life. The negative actions warn us vividly.

But when we follow Jesus, we get tastes of the liberty that crowns our spiritual achievements. We are delivered from what was holding us back from greater positive attainments. Whenever ungodliness is present or potential, the possibility of liberty is always implicit as the reward for getting it right. And there is something inherently joyous in the exercise of liberty.

The next chapter is dedicated to diverse tastes of joy.

Questions and Invitations

- List three positive aspects of religious tradition and three aspects of Jesus's new wine, the religion of the spirit, that we need more of today.

- Think of a personal growth need in your life now. It would involve one or more areas of Jesus's wilderness decisions: material, spiritual, and everything in between. What decision(s) would be most helpful? Imagine an assignment to mobilize your powers on this situation for a couple months, and see what happens. Notice your tastes of liberty as you are delivered step by step from the human tendencies in the direction of evil and sin.

10
Finding Joy in Life

IN ONE SENTENCE, Jesus revealed another aspect of his mission, his life, and the life of his followers. "I came that they may have life and have it abundantly" (Jn 10:10). "Abundantly" implies an overflow that is more than enough to barely get by. Abundant living for Jesus was centered on, but not narrowly focused on, spiritual things. Growing up with him is a holistic adventure.

The Son of Man was a master of an all-encompassing art of living. Jesus was fresh, alive, down-to-earth, imaginative, original, spontaneous, creative, vividly expressive, good-humored, and joyous.

When he urged, "Be of good cheer," Jesus was likely revealing his own overall disposition (Jn 16:33). He also would have found this attitude in Proverbs: "A merry heart does good like a medicine"; "A merry heart makes a cheerful countenance and is a continual feast" (17:22 and 15:13). This chapter focuses on the feeling of joy—which is roughly synonymous with good cheer—and supplements the joys scattered throughout the book. The reader may wish to review the end of chapter 3. A comment on two teachings previously mentioned: "The Father himself loves you" and "It is your Father's good pleasure to give you the kingdom" (Jn 16:27; Lk 12:32). Joy and kindred feelings can be touchingly evoked without being mentioned. If we read these teachings with a heart of stone, we miss the affective dimension that is essential to a truly receptive to Jesus's words; he spoke to the whole personality.

In general, I regard joy as a response to beauty. In chapter 7, we illustrated truth, beauty, and goodness, which engage our thinking, feeling, and doing on spiritual, intellectual, and material levels. In this chapter, we consider Jesus's responses on the levels of nature, the arts, spiritual experience, and gospel work.

Beauty in Nature

We can enter into Jesus's joy by participating in experiences similar to his. The curiosity of the child in each of us discovers in nature much to appreciate. At least by his teens, Jesus would have known the changing moods of the Sea of Galilee, the reliable stability of the nearby mountains, and the pleasing appearance of fields, flocks, and watered gardens.

Jesus would have appreciated the poetry of the sun and the stars in Psalm 19.

> The heavens are telling the glory of God,
>   and the firmament proclaims his handiwork.
> Day to day pours forth speech,
>   and night to night declares knowledge.

> There is no speech, nor are there words;
> their voice is not heard;
> yet their voice goes out through all the earth
> and their words to the end of the world.
> In the heavens he has set a tent for the sun,
> which comes out like a bridegroom from his wedding canopy,
> and like a strong man runs its course with joy.
> Its rising is from the end of the heavens
> and its circuit to the end of them,
> and nothing is hid from its heat.

The psalm gives voice to expressive qualities in nature. It reflects qualities of the Creator (his glory, craftsmanship, expressiveness, and knowledge) and the author's imagination (a bridegroom running across the heavens with strength and joy).

Jesus rejoiced in the Creator's handiwork. He drew his disciples' attention to beauty in nature: "Consider the lilies how they grow. They do not labor or spin. Yet I tell you, even Solomon in all his glory was not clothed like one of these" (Lk 12:27). In this context, to spin means to prepare thread for weaving cloth. In addition, Jesus delighted in observing how the Creator made provision for all living things. "Consider the ravens: They neither sow nor reap, they have no storehouse nor barn; and yet God feeds them" (Lk 12:24). Jesus's appreciation for birds and other non-human animals suggests that they were not created merely for humans.

Finally, Jesus's entire being manifested a naturalness that was grounded in being at home in nature. During much of his public career as a teacher, Jesus was homeless. He spent forty days alone in the wilderness. Spreading the message with his disciples, he walked all over Palestine and beyond.

The Arts

The perfect bridge between the Master's art of living and particular arts is a metaphor that Jesus would have enjoyed from First Isaiah: "The Lord is my strength and my song" (Is 12:2 RSV). Strength in life comes primarily from being centered in God; and the very thought of God as our song is so beautiful that I refuse to come up with a comment on it.

In the practical arts, Jesus was skilled in carpentry. In the fine arts, he put his unforgettable touch on storytelling. His parable of the talents portrays the joy of rewards for trustworthy individuals who invest their gifts in a wise and profitable way for the kingdom: "Well done, good and trustworthy servant; you have been trustworthy in a few things, I will put you in charge of many things; enter into the joy of your master" (Mt 25:21, slightly altered). Jesus, the joyful Master, gave us gifts, to begin with, his life and teachings. And we enter into his joy when we are creative—intelligent and productive—in working with these gifts. One way to enter into the joy of the Master is to study his parables and create some of our own to use.

The fun arts include play, sports, and humor. A merry heart has a sense of humor. This is worth emphasizing because it is easy to overlook this flavor of joy in Jesus. He asked, "Why do you see the speck in your neighbor's eye, but do not notice the log in your own eye?" (Mt 7:3). Exaggeration carried to impossible extremes is a mark of comedy.

Many of us are familiar with the phrase "wolves in sheep's clothing"; but in the first century, it would have been comical for his hearers to envision it (Mt 7:15). Taken out of context, the funniest of all Jesus's images was his criticism of Pharisees who "strain out a gnat but swallow a camel" (Mt 23:24). Some of his enemies were extremely careful not to consume even the slightest bit of food that was forbidden as "unclean." But these same Pharisees grossly polluted themselves by ignoring spiritual essentials. As a means of critique, in some settings, humor makes people receptive to otherwise unwelcome lessons.[21]

Joy in Spiritual Work

One of the greatest duties, privileges, and joys of being a follower of Jesus is doing spiritual work. Jesus had sent out seventy evangelists to teach and preach and heal (Lk 10:1–24). They came back rejoicing and reported their deeds of power in restoring suffering persons to wholeness. The Son of God cautioned them not to rejoice in their amazing successes, but to stay centered on what was even greater: "Rejoice that your names are written in heaven." In other words, their eternal life was assured, something greater than even their spiritual work.

Listening to these reports, Jesus was deeply moved because of how he saw the Creator working in the evangelists. His insight carries an essential message for us all. "He rejoiced in the Holy Spirit and said, 'I thank you, Father, Lord of heaven and earth, because you have hidden these things from the wise and the intelligent and have revealed them to infants; yes, Father, for such was your gracious will'" (Mt 11:25).

When Jesus spoke of "the wise and the intelligent," he seems to have been referring to persons who were intellectually gifted, well-educated, and wise in limited ways. From them were hidden spiritual wisdom and the power to do spiritual work. Their mental gifts and accomplishments were no substitute for dynamic faith. By contrast, the seventy generally lacked intellectual brilliance and worldly wisdom; and Jesus rejoiced in the evidence that ordinary beginners (infants) can do powerful work as gospel messengers.

Jesus's greatest teaching about the joy of successful gospel work is this parable:

> Which one of you, having a hundred sheep and losing one of them, does not leave the ninety-nine in the wilderness and go after the one that is lost until he finds it? When he has found it, he lays it on his shoulders and rejoices. And when he comes home, he calls together his friends and neighbors, saying to them, "Rejoice with me, for I have found my lost sheep." Just so, I tell you, there will be more joy in heaven God over one sinner who repents than over ninety-nine righteous persons who need no repentance (Lk 15:4–7).

This parable expresses the most thoroughgoing affirmation of the unimaginably great value of an individual. The shepherd rejoices. He calls friends and neighbors to rejoice. Likewise, there is joy in heaven over the infinitely loved one who was lost, then found, then led back to the circles of a loving community. No doubt the person who was saved sensed the joy of being welcomed home by persons seen and unseen.

We can enter into the beauty of Jesus's joy by sharing in this work: leading those who are lost to find their way home to the family of God. Some readers may think, "I'll go for most of these other joys, but I'll leave the joy of evangelism to others." This whole book can be read as an effort to entice these readers into the field.

Closing Comments

Jesus revealed an aspect of his personal life, an essential facet of his mission, and a great gift that he wanted us to share—abundant living—which is spiritually centered and all-inclusive in its scope.

Jesus's natural, good-humored, and creative art of living involved his whole personality embracing the whole of life.

We have considered abundant living in terms of various joys stimulated by the beauties of nature, the arts, and spiritual work. We enter into Jesus's joys by savoring them and by doing things similar to what he did. We can savor what is past, what is going on in the present, and what we anticipate in the future.

However, some of the examples reviewed here are challenging. Entering into Jesus's joy is not like going to a feast and simply loading up on desserts. There are entry-level joys and advanced joys on the divine path for each one of us as we find the way through beatitudes, other teachings, and stages in Jesus's life.

Fortunately, joy lights the way and encourages us step by step. Again I imagine Jesus saying with Isaiah, "My soul shall rejoice in the love of my God, for he has clothed me with the garments of salvation and has covered me with the robe of his righteousness" (Is 61:10). In other words, the prophet is savoring the deeply meaningful and satisfying gifts of God.

Finally, in living that is abundant, liberated, and joyous, God's spirit within finds fuller expression through us. In this way, we reveal God. And when we are truly following Jesus, we reveal him, too.

Questions and Invitations

- What is your concept of abundant living?
- What brings you joy? Do you ever take time to savor joy before, during, and after an event occurs?
- Which of your joys overlap with those of Jesus? Are there joys of Jesus in which you have little or no interest?
- How do you spread joy? How could you spread more of it?

Part II
THE SON OF MAN TEACHES HIS ORIGINAL MESSAGE

We now turn toward the second part of this book. Part I set forth living *faith*; Part II explores living *truth,* which we find in the concepts of the kingdom of God and the family of God. Part I refers to God as Father and Parent; Part II has a chapter on the fatherhood and motherhood of God. Part I introduced love; Part II has a chapter on what it means to love God with all our heart, soul, mind, and strength. Part I has focused largely on the individual; Part II goes into making neighborly love real by forgiving and serving others. Part I considered prayer and varieties of spiritual experience; Part II culminates with chapters on love, mercy, and service. Part I introduced being spirit-born; Part II leads toward being spirit-taught.

11
How Jesus Taught Living Truth

JESUS'S WAY OF teaching was a natural part of his way of living. The human Jesus lived the truth to such an extent that living truth became part of who he was. Great things happen when living faith (receptive and active) encounters living truth. This is how we become spirit-born.

To become spirit-taught, we need to develop further our receptivity to living truth, which manifests some of the qualities that Jesus had. He was alive, free, and responsive to the individuals and groups he was with and their ever-changing situations. By contrast, as we read what Jesus taught, sometimes our intellect gets in the way. Jesus's teachings were not designed to appeal especially to intellectual and religious elites; they were for everyone. Jesus avoided definitions, commentaries, and explanations. He provided guidance that met others' needs without saying too much.

To learn more of how and what Jesus taught will help us to better discern living truth. We briefly introduce Jesus's way of teaching in this chapter. This prepares us for the next one, where we encounter two major examples plus the concept of living truth.

Exercising Particular Virtues Based on Truths: An Example

Jesus taught by spontaneously expressing the qualities of the character that he had developed. An instructive teaching episode took place during the last week of Jesus's life, when some of his enemies tried to get him in trouble by asking a trick question.

> Then the Pharisees went and plotted to entrap him in what he said. So they sent their disciples to him, along with the Herodians, saying, "Teacher, we know that you are sincere, and teach the way of God in accordance with truth, and show deference to no one; for you do not regard people with partiality. Tell us, then, what you think. Is it lawful to pay taxes to the emperor, or not?" But Jesus, aware of their malice, said, "Why are you putting me to the test, you hypocrites? Show me the coin used for the tax." And they brought him a denarius. Then he said to them, "Whose head is this, and whose title?" They answered, "The emperor's." Then he said to them, "So give to the emperor what belongs to the emperor and to God what belongs to God." When they heard this, they were amazed; and they left him and went away (Mt 10:16).

The trap set for Jesus posed a dilemma. If he simply said, "Yes, it is lawful to pay the taxes," it could offend his supporters, who intensely resented them. If he simply said, "No, it is not lawful," his enemies could complain to the Roman governor, Pilate, that Jesus was inciting rebellion.

Many of Jesus's hearers knew what it was like to live under rulers who taxed them, and they knew that they could not get away with resisting taxes. Paying them was necessary for survival. Jesus's response to the question transformed an either/or dilemma into a both/and solution. His questioners simply walked away, not angry, but amazed.

In this interaction, Jesus showed the following virtues, which I associate with truths that Jesus lived. Jesus's *poise* in this potentially tense situation enabled him to expose hypocrisy *fearlessly* in a single sentence. Truth: there is nothing to fear. Then, *free of antagonism*, he proceeded in a manner that was *intelligent* and *wise*. Truths: enemies are siblings; and if we reason together, it is remarkable what we can do in God. He was *compassionate* toward those who paid heavy taxes while being *strong* in insisting that we worship God alone. Truths: we can be compassionate as God is compassionate; and if a ruler would force us to worship a false god, we have the free-will option to lay down our lives and give worship to God alone.

In so doing, Jesus showed philosophical and practical cleverness that amazed his conversation partners. Truth: there is always a divine way forward no matter what the situation may be.

What Jesus Did by the Way He Spoke

Living truth is active in spiritually productive ways. We all do different things by the various ways in which we use language. If

I say, "I forgive you," then you are forgiven. If the Son of Man says, "Your sins are forgiven," then God has forgiven your sins. Jesus did not use language in a premeditated, manipulative sense, but as a spontaneous way of relating. Consider a few examples.

Jesus gave promises, for example, in the beatitudes. Taking the first beatitude to heart establishes the basis for confidence and trust in the other beatitudes and in divine promises generally (Mt 5:3–12). The humble child of God, sincerely poor in spirit, who truly receives the kingdom experiences happiness now—in personal, spiritual experience. Every day of living as a child of God and a follower of Jesus renews this happiness. A general truth of divine promises is that if you satisfy the condition, the blessing is on the way.

And Jesus gave warnings, which protect his followers by informing them of the consequences of wrongdoing or to alert them to dangers connected with their mission. For example, we are called to work for spiritual unity among the family of Jesus's followers: "A kingdom divided against itself is laid waste" (Mt 12:25).

Jesus asked many questions, based on the truth that we can make discoveries for ourselves and help others to do the same. "Why do you call me 'Lord, Lord' and not do what I command?" (Lk 6:46).

Jesus combined teachings that were clear and direct with vivid images and parables. The parables engage the senses, stimulate the imagination, move the heart, challenge the mind, and uplift the soul. Truth engages our entire personality.[22]

Jesus's overall way of teaching illustrates living truth. The small portions of truth that he gave were never exactly the same. They did not all fit smoothly together in a neat intellectual system. The differences between them set up creative tensions in the hearers' minds. This is one way that living truth works to provoke fresh insight. It is close enough to what we already believe that we do not immediately reject it, and new enough to stimulate living faith to stretch in order to understand it.

A final example is that Jesus taught by commanding, for example, "You shall love the Lord your God with all your heart, and with all your soul, and with all your mind, and with all your strength. . . . And you shall love your neighbor as yourself" (Mk 12:28–31). If we could have seen and heard Jesus, we would realize that when Jesus commanded, he was doing other things at the same time. In this case, he was also:

- Exercising his authority as a leader and teacher in the kingdom
- Treating us as family and thus revealing the kingdom as a family
- Revealing God's love for us
- Sharing the top priorities in his own life
- Expressing the heart of spirituality for us all
- Empowering us by his faith in us, and in what we can do and be
- Drawing us into dynamic relation with him
- Calling us to treat all others in an appropriately loving way
- Implying that good comes from obeying the commandments and that unwelcome consequences result from disobeying them
- Bringing assurance of divine support every step of the way
- Filling with joy the receptive persons who are present with him

The living truth of Jesus's way of proclaiming these commandments silently accomplishes the doing of many other things that are related.

In all these ways, Jesus was a master teacher. I also regard him as *the Master* and refer to him as such (Jn 13:13, Lk 17:13). To avoid misunderstanding, let me clarify that this title does not imply that his followers are slaves. Indeed, he said, "I am among you as one who serves." To be a servant in this sense is fully compatible with the dignity of serving as Jesus did (Lk 22:27).

Summary and Transition

Reviewing this chapter, we can harvest some ideas and ideals for our own practice. Jesus's qualities of character and ways of teaching show us the way to be and to teach others. Increasingly we can become:

- Wise in the presence of enemies, and free of antagonism
- Poised and fearless
- Intelligent and wise
- Compassionate and strong
- Clever in logic and in practice

And we can:

- Express divine promises in our own words, not only by quoting from the Bible

- Teach divine promises, warn, and ask questions
- Share parables that we have created
- Give commands that are anchored in our experience of obeying them
- Speak not based on a system of intellectual ideas, but in the living spiritual relationship with persons and groups in response to a particular situation

As we practice and grow, these qualities and ways of teaching become a natural part of how we live. We are now beginning to teach, or continuing to teach, living truth in a way that exemplifies living truth.

Now we are prepared for the next chapter, where we inquire into two of Jesus's most important examples of living truth: the kingdom of God and the family of God.

Questions and Invitations

- Pick a truth that Jesus taught that you would like to teach. What particular virtues or qualities do you think Jesus exercised in teaching this truth? As you find situations in which ways to practice, try also to express one or more of these strengths.

- Prepare to teach the commandments to love God and the neighbor. Compare the many things that Jesus also did when he taught the first two love commands. Contemplate these things and see how some of them might uplift your teaching.

12

The Living Truth of the Kingdom of God and the Family of God

IN A WORLD that presents a mix of truths, half-truths, errors, deliberate distortions, and outright lies, truth is a basic value. It orients daily living and puts mind and soul on solid ground.

Although God is beyond human understanding, truth is a value that we can comprehend to a significant degree. For those hungry to base their lives on truth, Jesus's teachings are a feast. He encouraged truth seekers with a promise: "Search, and you will find" (Mt 7:7). As we embrace what we find of divine truth, we become spirit-taught.

As the previous chapter made clear, when Jesus taught, the quality of who he was and the ways in which he interacted with his hearers make him our prime example of living truth. As Zacchaeus showed, when living faith meets living truth, the result can be life-changing (Lk 19:1–10).

In this chapter, we first consider the two main examples of concepts of living truth in the teaching of Jesus: the kingdom of God and the family of God. These two concepts overlap. Then we explore the concept of living truth itself. Some readers may understand more easily if they start with this chapter's last section.

The Kingdom of God

In the gospel of the kingdom, Jesus spoke to people's needs for spiritual insight into widely varying circumstances and aspects of life. I emphasize these differences by presenting the gospel in pairs of contrasting sides. Each side illustrates the divine response to persons or groups who need a specific truth at a particular time.

- The kingdom of God is the family of God, those who have become the sons and daughters of God, receiving the kingdom as a little child—in humble and trusting faith. I sometimes use the term "kingdom family" to refer to the kingdom of God as something one can join. Jesus's life and teachings redefine the concept of God as our Father, and what it means to be a member of his family.

- On the other hand, "the kingdom of God is within you" (Lk 17:20). In the divine spirit, God is present in the individual.

- Jesus proclaimed that "the kingdom of God is at hand"—now (Mk 1:15). On the other hand, the kingdom of heaven is in the future. We pray, "Your kingdom come, your will be done on earth as in heaven" (Mt 6:10). This vision of the rule of God which comes to full fruition in our planetary destiny may take thousands of years to become a reality. But on the individual level, Jesus has already shown us the way.

- For those with receptive faith, the kingdom is easy to enter. "Happy are the poor in spirit, for theirs is the kingdom of heaven" (Mt 5:3, Acts 3:47). "Knock and the door will be opened to you" (Mt 7:7).

- On the other hand, the kingdom is a moving target. "The kingdom of heaven is like a net that was thrown into the sea and caught fish of every kind; when it was full, they drew it ashore, sat down, and put the good into baskets but threw out the bad" (Mt 13:47–48). All persons of faith who knock on the door of the kingdom are welcomed in. But to remain takes growth, which requires effort, perhaps severe testing; and some give up along the way, say 'no' to life as their final answer, and uproot the beautiful salvation that they had received.

- The kingdom is brimming with joy and happiness. "The kingdom of heaven is like a treasure hidden in a field, which someone found and then hid; then in his joy he goes and sells all that he has and buys that field" (Mt 13:44).

- On the other hand, followers have a choice regarding whether to progress at a more gradual rate or to follow Jesus in the selfless service of "fulfilling all righteousness" (Mt 3:15), which leads more readily to persecution and death. To those who suffer for their loyalty to the truth that Jesus taught, he said, "Rejoice and be exceedingly glad." The same thing happened to earlier prophets. "Your reward is great in heaven" (Mt 5:11–12). This implies, "You should see them now!" Indeed, for *everyone in the family of faith—all who say 'YES' with their lives*, there is more joy after this life than during it.

When I speak of *the family of faith*, I mean to include in my concept of the kingdom persons of other religions and other individual believers in whom faith in God (or a functional equivalent) is alive and well. Many of Jesus's teachings overlap with those found in other religions. It is not surprising that Jesus could celebrate the faith of a Roman centurion who was not Jewish (Mt 8:5–10).

The Family of God

We have seen that, to begin with, the family of God are those who have entered the kingdom by faith. But one of the ways that Jesus's teachings manifest living truth is that the same key term can have different meanings in different contexts. To see this, consider the question, "Who is in the family of God?" In addition to the kingdom family, there are three more answers to this question.

Jesus once said, "Who are my mother and sisters and brother? Whoever does the will of my Father in heaven" (Mt 12:50). Here to be in Jesus's family involves more than being born of the spirit. Family members must do God's will. This idea also overlaps with the kingdom of God, since we need to stay in the kingdom by growing, which includes doing the will of God.

Jesus also taught, "Happy are the peacemakers, for they shall be called the children of God" (Mt 5:10). This is also a higher standard than entry-level belief. The future tense here may imply that our status as children of God is a reality that is eternally sealed only in heaven. If this idea is right, then none of us is fully and finally certified as a child of God.

The last answer to the question of who is in the family of God includes all persons. If God is the Creator of each person—and no one else is creating persons—then everyone is a child of God. This inclusive concept is implied in many important teachings of Jesus.

- "You shall love your neighbor as yourself" (Mk 12:31, Lv 19:18). The neighbor is anyone who can be affected by our action or inaction.

- "Do to others as you want others to do to you" (Lk 6:31, Mt 7:12). This rule is stated in many different versions; but, simply put, it is the most universal moral principle on the planet.

- "Forgive us our debts as we forgive our debtors" (Mt 6:12). Whom are we to forgive? Only other believers?

- "To the extent that you did it to one of the least of my brothers and sisters, you did it to me" (Mt 25:40). Did Jesus care about how his followers treated one another, but not so much about how we treated others? On the contrary. He said that his mission was "to seek out and to save the lost" (Lk 19:10).

- "By this everyone will know that you are my disciples, if you love one another" (Jn 13:34–35). Can we accomplish our mission to the world if our love is directed mainly to fellow believers?

This next example is the most direct support for what I regard as the hub that can serve as a foundation for the other truths of Jesus's gospel.

Few people see their enemies as family, especially in the midst of a conflict where one's life is at stake. But during the last week of his life, at the high point of the conflict with the religious leaders, Jesus made a dramatic statement which included all persons in the family of God. He gave his final talk in the Temple to a crowd containing both followers and enemies. The Son of Man told everyone, "You are all brothers," and "You all have one Father" (Mt 23:8–9). With these simple, clear, direct words of life, Jesus proclaimed the heart of the message he lived and taught: the fatherhood of God and the brotherhood of man.

These two teachings pioneer the way for Jesus's other gospel teachings; they say more about our Parent or humankind or both. Even the teaching of Jesus as the Son of God can be interpreted as Jesus revealing the fatherhood of God and also as showing each of us how to live as a child of our Parent and as a sibling in the universal family.

The concept of the universal family is a bulwark against the "I-am-better-than-they-are" attitude. To counter this attitude, consider first that many persons of faith who are not followers of Jesus are closer to God than many professed followers of Jesus. Second, Jesus was especially interested in reaching out to persons who were not persons of faith. Third, Jesus revealed a Father who loves us all—equally and infinitely.

Living Truth

Jesus said, "You shall know the truth, and the truth shall make you free" (Jn 8:32). This section gathers some images and thoughts to suggest something of how this happens.

As stated previously, the living God puts down the ladder of living truth that reaches down from heaven to earth. Coming from this high source, truth is eternally dependable. But for all its stability, truth cannot be fixed and frozen. God approaches unique individuals in particular ways that they can understand, so not everyone receives the same expression of a particular truth. In addition, God inspires prophets who address large numbers of people living in their time. To some extent, each generation has its own problems in spiritual growth. This is another reason that divine truth is flexible in its expression.

Think of the familiar story of the elephant described differently by people who are blindfolded and touching only the trunk or tail, or only a tusk, ear, or leg. We smile at how limited each description is. Truth sponsors all insights available from every perspective. Truth meets us where we are and takes us further. Often it leads us around to where others are, so that we can look at the elephant from there. Truth is many-sided.

Looking into a kaleidoscope, we see mirrors and pieces of colored glass that give lovely, changing reflections of light and color. In the interwoven aspects of Jesus's many-sided message, we see the beauty of truth in the way the Master spontaneously taught gems to this individual and that group. And we see the goodness of truth in his way of drawing on his rich message to give his hearers what would best serve them. This beauty and goodness show the life of truth.

Living truth moves like a reel of film on a movie projector. One can pause the movie at a particular frame and take time to think about it. Likewise, we can write down and reflect on particular truths. But we humans cannot formulate and define living truth.

Living truth eventually leads us into all truth, scientific and philosophical as well as spiritual. All truth is God's truth. When we are willing to follow wherever it leads, and willing to obey the truth, we are spirit-led (see Part III); and Jesus's message does its work at a new level. It is not like an abstract idea. In the mind and soul, truth is more a *who* than a *what*.

Now we are in a position to understand Jesus's assurance, "You shall know the truth, and the truth shall make you free" (Jn 8:32). This liberation comes about when living truth meets living faith. Truth works like a time-release vitamin. Jesus usually gave truth in small portions. If one of these "capsules" speaks to a spiritual difficulty that is holding you back, you take notice and pay closer attention. Truth gets started right away, usually in the mind. As you take time to stop and ponder, as you let it sink in, truth moves into your soul. It keeps on releasing its goodness, leading us into the presence of the God whose spirit dwells within. From on high, from close at hand, and from this spiritual center within, divine truth liberates you to enter into, or advance in, the life of faith.

Summary and Transition

We have considered the living truth in Jesus's teachings of the kingdom of God in four pairs of contrasting truths that do not contradict each other when we grasp their meanings.

Next we identified four meanings of the family of God, beginning with the kingdom of God, which I sometimes call the kingdom family. Extra support was brought forth for the idea of the family of God in which each human person is a member; this I sometimes call the universal family.

Finally, we considered the concept of living truth. It is sturdy and reliable because it comes from God. At the same time it is flexible or in motion. This is because it contains many ideas, and it moves from one meaning or level to another. Several images convey the flexibility, including a ladder, an elephant, a kaleidoscope, a reel of film, and a time-release capsule. In the light of these images, we can understand why "The truth makes you free." Truth can bring liberty because it is more like a 'who' than a 'what.'

In briefest summary, Jesus usually spoke of the kingdom by using the language of family. Thus, entering the kingdom implies becoming a member in the family of God. But Jesus's teachings also imply another, all-inclusive meaning of the term "family of God." God is the Parent of everyone. No one else is creating persons. So we are all siblings.

Once we recognize living truth in Jesus's gospel, we sense that it can and will continue to adapt and expand to meet each generation's new spiritual needs. This portrayal of the living truth of Jesus's gospel extends into the next chapter, which focuses on religious language and gender.

Questions and Invitations

- What are the advantages of speaking about primary spiritual reality in terms of the kingdom of God?

- What are the advantages of speaking in terms of the family of God?

- Jesus tended to speak about the kingdom using the language of family. Was he combining conservative and liberal approaches? How do you think he would speak about these realities with different groups today?

13
Revealing God as Father and Mother

WE EACH have our own story about how we developed our own individual way of speaking to and about God. If we find ourselves in a polarized society, this can make it harder for many of us to give voice to the meanings and values that are most important to us. But no matter how skillfully or awkwardly we paddle through the rapids of choosing language to speak with others, it is good to attain our own insight regarding the truth of some of the alternatives. Here we have another adventure with living truth.

The Fatherhood of God

In Jesus's life and teachings, the fatherhood of God became living truth. To understand what he was doing, we first look back four thousand years to the beginning of Jewish tradition. God was revealed as having sovereign will. Faith in the all-powerful and righteous Creator of the heavens and the earth—one God—replaced the alternative, plural gods of lesser stature. The classical monotheistic emphasis on the unity of God contrasted, for example, with the Greek gods. They were personal but were originally created in the image of human beings. The concept of Zeus, king of the gods, evolved; but sometimes the gods' behavior exhibited human vices.[23]

As we see in Jesus, the clear truth of monotheism serves as an ideal foundation. Jesus's life and his original gospel were God-centered. Classical monotheism is also of great value in our relations with religions other than Christianity. Therefore, a Trinitarian theology with its resources for recognizing the motherhood of God should not simply replace classical monotheism in our daily faith and in evangelism.

But whether or not we describe our experience in these terms, I believe that we experience both fatherly and motherly love in God. Moses and Isaiah referred to God as father (Dt 32:6, Is 63:16); Moses compared God with a mother bird gently lifting up her little ones. "As an eagle stirs up its nest, and hovers over its young; it spreads its wings, takes them up, and bears them aloft on its pinions" (Dt 32:11). And God spoke through the prophet Isaiah: "As a mother comforts her child, so I will comfort you" (Is 66:13). In my opinion, vocabulary for God's love in the Bible suggests that the nurturing, merciful, motherly aspects of love are also commonly felt. Proverbs 8:22–36 is a source for the tradition of Divine Wisdom, Sophia, as female and as God's first created partner in forming the heavens and the earth.

Part of the Master's mission as I see it was to reveal the *personality* of God; and he wanted people to share as much as possible the close personal relationship that he enjoyed with God. He could have said, "God is my Father and your Grandfather." Instead, in a brotherly way, he referred to God as *our* Father. Someone who wants to find God as their Father can simply relate to God with the receptive and active faith of a child.

Is the Word "Father" for God a Metaphor?

Many persons around the globe today regard the father concept of God as sexist. But most people in the debate unite on two things. First, righteous indignation about the fact that untold numbers of persons have horrible memories of an abusive father. We do well to join in supporting victims, promoting justice and rehabilitation for abusers, and working for a better world for families.

Another thing that almost everyone in the debate agrees on is that the father concept of God is a metaphor. This is a use of language like that of Moses in calling God "the rock" (Dt 32:4). The primary meaning of this term is visible rocks in nature. God has stability "like a rock" but God is not, properly speaking, a rock. If the word "Father" for God is a metaphor, then Jesus would have had biological or sociological images in mind which he projected onto God as the basis for calling God "Father."

A different use of language is illustrated by saying that God is good. God's goodness is the source and pattern for goodness in the creature. A human being becomes good by entering into, or participating in, God's goodness. This is not a metaphor but technically speaking an "analogy." But why should we assume that the father concept of God is like calling God "the rock" and not like calling God "good"?

If Jesus knew God better than any other human being, we can choose to regard *Jesus's proclamation of the Father as a top-down revelation of relationship, not a bottom-up projection of the image of a biological or sociological male onto God.* I further believe that *Jesus primarily taught the fatherhood of God, not in contrast with the motherhood of God, but in contrast with the idea of God as a remote and powerful king.*

Without revelation from a divine source, we would indeed be projecting human images and ideas onto God. I imagine that, in the far future, when we are "face-to-face" with the Creator in heaven, we will understand how inadequate it is to project the image of a biological and sociological male onto God. I also believe that we will understand why Jesus chose to use the father concept to express his revelation of the Creator's personality to human beings.

Jesus's Possible Expressions of the Motherhood of God

I believe that Jesus deliberately prepared the way for the eventual realization of the motherhood of God. By what he said and did, he also planted spiritual seeds for the social realization of the equality of women with men plus the eventual end of patriarchy and the recognition of the motherhood of God.

Jesus could well have anticipated that there would be increasing numbers of persons who would need assurance of the motherhood of God. Then they could accept God as fair and feel welcomed into the family. Consider what Jesus said in this regard: "To what should I compare the kingdom of God? It is like yeast that a woman took and hid in three measures of flour until all of it was leavened" (Lk 13:20–21). As leaven spreads through a loaf of bread to make it rise, truth and love will eventually pervade humankind. The woman symbolizes the role of God or Jesus in the kingdom, which has implications for women's access to functioning as religious leaders. Jesus was also lifting up daily work such as preparing meals as meaningful service comparable to customary roles for men—and potentially implying that child-rearing is work for men to share in, too.

"What woman having ten silver coins, if she loses one of them, does not light a lamp, sweep the house, and search carefully until she finds it? When she has found it, she calls together her friends and neighbors, saying, 'Rejoice with me, for I have found the coin that I had lost.' Just so, I tell you, there is joy in the presence of the angels of God over one sinner who repents" (Lk 15:8–10). The woman symbolizes God or Jesus or anyone who works with God, painstakingly seeking to find how to reach someone who is lost. Each person is infinitely precious.

Jesus even compared himself to a mother. "Jerusalem, Jerusalem, the city that kills the prophets and stones those who are sent to it! How often have I desired to gather your children together as a hen gathers her chicks under her wings, and you were not willing!" (Mt 23:37). What experience lies behind this lament? Jesus must have spent time observing chickens, noticing how the mother hen gives comfort and safety to her baby chicks when their welfare requires that she gather them under her wings. It is possible that he identified with those hens. Some animal behaviors foreshadow the tender care that human beings can give as we become like God.

Jesus also stood up for women on a number of occasions. His enemies brought before him a woman who had been caught in the act of adultery. They claimed that Moses had commanded them to kill her by throwing stones at her; and they asked Jesus what he had to say about that. They suspected that Jesus's compassion would lead him into conflict with the law, giving them an excuse to report him to authorities. In silence, Jesus wrote something in the sand in front of each of her accusers. They continued to press their question, and he responded.

> He straightened up and said to them, "Let him who is without sin among you be the first to throw a stone at her." And once more he bent down and wrote on the ground. In response to what he said, they went away one by one. Jesus was left alone with the woman standing before him. He stood up and said to her, "Woman, where are they? Has no one condemned you?" She said, "No one, Lord." And Jesus said, "Neither do I condemn you" (Jn 8:3–11).

Note that in Jesus's culture, to call her "woman" was an entirely proper and respectful way to address an adult female.

When his life on earth was drawing to a close, Jesus visited with his friends Mary and Martha. Mary took the opportunity to anoint him with very expensive, sweet-smelling oil. Judas Iscariot voiced what others were thinking: he criticized her for not giving the money to the poor. Jesus strongly defended her:

> Leave her alone. Why do you trouble her? She has done a beautiful thing to me. For you always have the poor with you, and whenever you want, you can do good for them. But you will not always have me. She has done what she could; she has anointed my body beforehand for burial. And truly, I say to you, wherever the gospel is

proclaimed in the whole world, what she has done will be told in memory of her (Mt 26:6–13).

The story appears in the other three gospels, as well (Mk 14:3–9, Lk 7:38–46, Jn 12:1–8).

About this last bit of information, I simply want to pose a question. We read in the Gospel of Luke that "Jesus went on through cities and villages, proclaiming and bringing the good news of the kingdom of God. And the twelve were with him, and also some women who had been healed . . . Mary, called Magdalene . . . and Joanna, the wife of Chuza, Herod's household manager, and Susanna, and many others, who provided for them out of their means" (Lk 8:3). Why is it so easy to assume that these women did no preaching, teaching, or other ministry?

The Holy Spirit as Our Mother

If we accept the fatherhood of God, and if we regard women and men as equally essential to revealing God, a question arises. Is it possible that the unity of God includes more than one personality? A revelation came to nineteenth-century preacher Rebecca Jackson:

> I saw that night, for the first time, a Mother in the Deity. This indeed was a new scene, a new doctrine to me. But I knowed when I got it, and I was obedient to the heavenly vision. . . . And was I not glad when I found that I had a Mother! And that night She gave me a tongue to tell it! The spirit of weeping was upon me, and it fell on all the assembly. And though they never

heard it before, I was made able by Her Holy Spirit of Wisdom to make it so plain that a child could understand it.[24]

I believe that God had a 'plan A' for theological progress in Jesus's time and place. Accordingly, Jesus seems to have wanted his followers first to find God the Father or to strengthen their bond with him. When this achievement was securely in place, his followers were next to recognize himself as the Son of God. When this loyalty was established, I believe that people were then to discover the Holy Spirit as our Mother. This sequence takes time—perhaps decades or generations—to accomplish in an enduring way in individuals, let alone large groups. If so, then it would explain why Jesus used indirect methods to convey the motherhood of God. When all the pieces of the Trinitarian puzzle are solidly in place in believer's heart, soul, mind, and strength, the result will be majestic.

The Mystery of God

A truth that almost everyone in the debate can agree on is that the infinite and eternal God is far beyond our finite, human capacity to comprehend. Thus, it is wise to humbly recognize our limits and leave room in our concept of God for mystery. The divine mystery is transcendent and awesome, spacious and lovely, warm and delicious. It invites us to relax in the thought that there is always much more to God than we can ever take in.

A sense of mystery is involved at the beginning of the prayer that Jesus taught: "Our Father, who is in heaven, hallowed be your name." Here the Son of Man used the profound word "name" in the singular. Jesus well knew that there are many names for God. I believe that what makes a name for God hallowed—sacred or holy—is that, when we use it meaningfully in a reverent attitude, it activates our relationship with God.

When Moses asked to know the name of the One who was calling him, simply put, God responded as "I AM" (Ex 3:14). This name is the primal beginning of the revelation of God as personal reality. I AM dwells forever in mystery. When we address the Creator, we are on holy ground. God says, "Be still and know that I am God" (Ps 46:10).

Comments, Summary, and Transition

I have claimed that the fatherhood of God is at the heart of Jesus's gospel. In this chapter I have gone as far as I can in giving reasons for my view. Jesus did not debate or argue for his teachings. He proclaimed the fatherhood of God, but he did not impose it. His concept is friendly and inviting. It does not require conformity from those who think, feel, and speak otherwise.

Because of widespread problems with the fatherhood of God today, I often treat this teaching as semi-advanced, not one to begin with. In many situations, it is wise to do what Jesus did most of the time: Keep it simple. Avoid needless controversy. Attribute all divine qualities and functions to God. I presented an alternative to the idea that Jesus's father concept of God was a metaphorical projection of an image of a biological or sociological male onto God. I regard Jesus's concept of God as our Father as a top-down revelation of the personality of God. Moreover, for Jesus, the primary defining contrast of the fatherhood of God is not with the motherhood of God but with God as a remote and powerful king.

To repeat what has been said earlier, countless God-knowing persons have used different names and developed great relationships with the Creator. The quality of our relationship is what matters most. And we are free to choose names for God that fit our experience.

In setting forth my ideas, I would like to believe that Jesus is cheering me on. But when I pray for those whose beliefs and practices differ from my own, I can also imagine them praying for persons like me. When I recall how easy it is to assume that one's own ways are better, I smile.

I observe that our spiritual progress is partly because of our beliefs and practices and partly in spite of them. Even when the beliefs are true and the actions correct, we may still need to grow in how we hold our beliefs and how we do things. Good relationships with one another are tremendously important to good relationships with our heavenly Parent(s). Fortunately, we do not need to agree intellectually in order to enjoy spiritual unity.

Regarding the motherhood of God, this chapter portrayed living truth with no fixed answers to apply in every situation. We recalled some qualities of classical monotheism that are still virtues today. Within the framework of that monotheism, Biblical vocabulary suggests that the nurturing, merciful, motherly aspects of divine love are also very commonly felt.

We also considered several texts which suggest that Jesus was keen to include women as equals and leaders in the kingdom family of God and as siblings in the universal family. This was followed by an account of a revelatory experience proclaiming the reality of a Mother in deity that can be interpreted as supporting the idea of the Holy Spirit as our Mother. The last topic was a reminder that the interests of the philosophical and theological intellect differ from the needs of the soul. As always with living truth, the aspect of mystery is present. Naming God, we are on holy ground.

Having considered religious language and gender, we turn now to begin a series of three chapters that focus on love and its outworking in forgiving and serving others.

Questions and Invitations

- What does the concept of the fatherhood of God mean to you? The motherhood of God?

- Do you find yourself affected by the debate about religious language for God? If not, what do you make of it? If so, how do you handle it? Does the concept of living truth help?

- Are you able to sustain a feeling and conviction of spiritual unity with persons whose approach to religious language differs from yours? On what basis do you do so? If you struggle at times, how do you succeed in gaining the attitude that reflects your entering into God's goodness?

14

Loving God and the Neighbor Wholeheartedly

Everything previously said in this book leads up to love, and everything that comes afterward flows from love.

From the teachings that Moses had given, Jesus selected and gave top priority to two laws of love. The first he called "the greatest commandment," and the second he said was "like it": "You shall love the Lord your God with all your heart, and with all your soul, and with all your mind, and with all your strength. A second is like it. You shall love your neighbor as yourself" (Mk 12:28–31, Mt 22:34–40, Lk 10:25–28; Dt 6:4–5, Lv 19:18).

Emphasizing these two commandments gave a needed focus for the religious lives of many of Jesus's Jewish followers. They had been burdened with pressure to obey hundreds of laws in the scriptures plus the oral law. This second collection of laws was also thought to be backed up by the authority of Moses and the power of the Creator. This interpretation instilled fear in many believers. In simplest terms, the Son of Man wanted to replace the religion of fear with the religion of love.

Focusing mainly on these two commandments could be liberating in the first century, but we need another liberation for the challenges involved today. The greatest commandments are rooted in the greatest truths: the fatherhood of God and the brotherhood of man, the parenthood of God and the siblinghood of humankind. Only love can motivate us to cooperate effectively to make our siblinghood a practical reality in this world.

Receiving God's love and returning it is the first circuit of love. Its beauty and truth empower us for *the second circuit—extending Godly love to the neighbor.* And getting active in the second circuit increasingly awakens us to the goodness and power of the first circuit.

The first circuit of love starts from God, the source of love.

Receiving God's Love

We have been told that God loves us. But believing it and experiencing it are two different things. I believe that Jesus wanted us to share as much as possible his experience of being loved by our Father and loving him in return.

God loved us first, before we had any idea of the Creator. The simplest way to experience God's love is to open ourselves with the trusting, receptive faith of a little child. God wants to fill us with love and has already sent God's spirit into our hearts to do this.

Some persons find it hard to allow God's love to come into them. For example, there may be a need to release bad feelings about our body and mind. When we look in the mirror, it is common to see some physical pluses and minuses. When we observe our minds, it is common to see some things that we feel good about and other things not so much. This human mix might not seem to fit with our idea that God truly loves us. But each of us is profoundly respected as a child of God and accepted and loved as who we are now.

The self we see in the mirror and experience in our minds is not the true and deeper self, the soul. The affection of people who truly know and love us is not based primarily on our qualities of body and mind. They love us for who we truly are.

Some people struggle to love themselves. If we give this stressful effort a vacation and dare to allow God's love in, we may discover something more soul-satisfying than what we had been striving for. We can let God's love reveal to us who we truly are.

The more we experience God's love for us, the more God becomes our *first love*. Imagine seeing your best friend and asking, "What can I do for you?" Your friend answers, "Just love me." You relax into the simplicity of natural, open, free relating. Affection comes over you, satisfying both you and your friend.

To each of us God gives all the love we can receive. And I believe that Jesus highlighted the love commandments partly because loving God and the neighbor enhances our capacity to receive divine love.

Loving God with All Our Heart, Soul, Mind, and Strength

With all our heart

Loving God begins in the heart. To love God with all our heart is to love wholeheartedly. This quality can be defined by contrast: not half-hearted, lukewarm, indecisive, or conflicted. Wholeheartedness is a sign that the whole personality is engaged.

If I am not also loving God with all my mind, soul, or strength, it will show up as a lack of wholeheartedness.

Some of Jesus's teachings enlighten us about the heart. To some Pharisees he said, "Isaiah prophesied rightly about you hypocrites, as it is written, 'This people honors me with their lips, but their hearts are far from me; in vain do they worship me . . .'" (Mk 7:6–7). Our heart is the seat of our motivation. If we say that we value someone or something, but our life does not show it, then our heart is actually longing for something else that competes with this value.

Jesus said, "Where your treasure is, there will be your heart also." Wealthy and greedy persons' hearts are chained to the bars of gold under their pillow. Divine truth is the treasure of a truth-loving heart. The same thing holds with a heart in love with divine beauty, and a person who hungers and thirsts for divine goodness.

Jesus's frank realism about the potential for evil in the human heart helps us face it honestly. Earlier, contrasting evil and sin with the way of life, we saw that the Master listed a dozen kinds of evil that come from the human heart (Mk 7:21–22, Mt 15:19). And God knows perfectly well that we are not going to totally overcome evil tendencies in this life. But we do not want to put up a chain-link fence around any area of our life and put up a sign: "Off limits to God." Neither did Jesus tell us to examine ourselves every night before bedtime and dig around looking for mud. Seek for mud, and there is always more to find.

Jesus placed emphasis on a positive approach. "Happy are the pure in heart, for they shall see God." The promise about seeing God is partly for the next life. But we can also experience a pure heart in this life, I propose, in three steps.

The first step is to nurture the goodness that is already present in the heart. Positive psychologist Barbara Fredrickson has discovered *a natural tendency for positive feelings in the heart to blossom and fill us, if we allow this to occur and encourage it.* Examples of positive emotions include gratitude, joy, awe, inspiration, serenity, interest, amusement, feeling good about oneself, and love.[25]

I believe that Fredrickson has found something of how the spirit of God works in the heart. What starts as a warm feeling can rise all the way to worship.

Philosophically, I think of body, mind, soul, and spirit as the parts of the human personality. *I regard the heart as including the emotions of mind and the feelings of soul—in response to values.* One way for the pure in heart to see God is to recognize divine values of truth, beauty, and goodness on all levels in our daily lives. For example, imagine seeing violets come up in the lawn in the spring, intellectually enjoying a performance by an Iranian-American stand-up comic whose comedy is clean, and having a taste-and-see spiritual experience of Jesus sitting (invisible) across the dinner table.

The second step is to deal with the unbeautifulness that from time to time arises in the heart. One simple and positive way is to allow this prayer to blossom and fill the heart: "Create in me, a clean heart, O God, and put in me a new and right spirit" (Ps 51:10). Soaking in this prayer increases our receptivity to the divine transformation that we cannot do for ourselves. As a result, we are empowered to take human steps to cooperate with our cleansing as we continue to seek growth in loving God with all our heart, soul, mind, and strength. We go forward with a happy, forgiven heart.

The third step is to rejoice in the divine mercy that gives us a pure heart to love God wholeheartedly. The Creator has designed our partnership so that a powerful decision can liberate us far more than we might have anticipated. Once we commit to loving God supremely, great things start to happen. When we pray for, and cooperate with, our transformation, God's spirit within can put unbeautifulness out of action. It is like skating on thick ice.

The deep and icy waters below do not in the least threaten our security. We are given a taste of being pure in heart. This is the sense in which we can love God with all our heart.

With all our soul

If I am right that the heart's feelings in response to values come in large measure from the soul, then much of what has been said about wholeheartedness and being pure in heart applies to the soul. For example, to love God with all our soul, we nurture the best in our inner life and allow it to blossom. We can "taste and see that the Lord is good" (Ps 34:8). The soul is the part of us which does that—perceives the presence of God and discerns divine goodness. On this path we have beautifully merciful tastes of whole-souled loving, and as we advance in faith, trust, and hunger for God's righteousness, things get better and better.

In my concept, the soul is a work in progress. A soul can be lost, hurt, torn, or even rebellious. And the soul can move from lost to found, from hurt to radiant, from torn to unified, and from rebellious to wholeheartedly in love with God. However, in my opinion, the soul is more the seat of positive feelings, whereas the mind, along with its great positive potentials, is usually more exposed to negative stimuli.

When we are being soulful, we are being authentic, who we truly are. Most of us, most of the time, are centered in our body and mind. But when we move into our soul, it is like shifting into a higher gear: less taxing on the engine and more effective in traveling down the road. It is more relaxing, less gripped by the mind's tensions, as we allow ourselves to come into that better place. This is our true self, our higher self—the soul. I put it this way. I *have* a mind and a body; the soul is who I *am*.

The soul is the enduring part of us which can survive into the next life. Jesus spoke of enemies who can "kill the body but cannot kill the soul" (Mt 10:20). The power of the soul was evident in Protestant reformer Martin Luther when he was brought before a theological tribunal. They tried to pressure him into renouncing some of his controversial teachings. With his life on the line, he replied stoutly, "Here I stand. I cannot do otherwise."[26] *That's* the soul speaking. Regardless of theological differences, martyrs in every century have shown the same quality of courage.

For many people, a major challenge in loving God is how to deal gracefully with the fact that love is commanded. The mind can be motivated to obey the commandments of our just and wise Sovereign in order to fulfill a duty. But the highest motivation is love. Psalm 19 gives us more than a taste of how an intellect with a complex awareness of duty can play a supportive role in loving God with all one's soul. I imagine the young Jesus nurturing his mind and soul on this passage and then seeing and hearing him later conducting a worship service and reading this selection.

> The law of the Lord is perfect,
> reviving the soul.
> The decrees of the Lord are sure,
> making wise the simple.
> The precepts of the Lord are right,
> rejoicing to the heart.
> The commands of the Lord are clear,
> enlightening the eyes.
> The fear of the Lord is pure,
> enduring forever.
> The ordinances of the Lord are true,
> and righteous altogether.

> They are more to be desired than gold,
> even much fine gold;
> sweeter also than honey,
> and drippings of the honeycomb.
> Moreover, by them is your servant warned;
> in keeping them there is great reward (Ps 19:7–11).

Through the author's words we feel a soul that is brimming with love for our just, wise, and loving Creator. The Psalm connects God's commandments with reviving the soul, wisdom and rejoicing, enlightening clarity, purity and permanence, truth and righteousness, the most desirable sweetness, warning and reward. In this context, "fear" refers to reverent respect and awe. God's law, decrees, precepts, commandments, and ordinances are not submitted to as demands backed up by threats. Rather, they are welcomed as revelations of the goodness of the God whose "steadfast love endures forever" (Ps 118:1).

An image may be helpful on the relation of mind and soul. Imagine driving on a winding and somewhat foggy road and coming to a sharp turn, where a curved mirror posted on the side of the road lets travelers see in a partial way what they can see better after the turn. The driver approaching the turn is like the mind, which is conscious of a partial reflection of what the soul sees. Like the driver who has passed the turn, the soul's perception of spirit is not perfectly clear, but it perceives more than what the mind sees.

With all our mind

For all the beauty of a soulful, poetic, love-saturated Psalm, the laws of love are still commandments. The Master did not say, "Try to love," "Do your best to love." Jesus commanded us to love because he knew that *we can*. Urgings that are too gentle merely beg for love; they lack the invigorating power of a divine command and the quality of love that motivates it. Free of harshness, divine commandments encourage us to persist when disappointments and difficulties arise. Doing our utmost wholeheartedly opens us to receive the fullness of what God is ready to do in us.

It is noteworthy that Jesus added "with all your mind." By contrast, Moses had commanded loving God "with all your heart and with all your soul and with all your might" (De 6:5). In the New Testament, only Mark—the least intellectually inclined gospel—includes this addition (Mk 12:28-31). I believe that Jesus was emphasizing a fuller concept of the human being; he was looking forward to a time when people would recognize that science and philosophy, for example, have a proper place in the intelligent and wise love of God.

In putting love into practice, we make daily decisions in our mind. To begin loving God with all our mind in a big way, we can give to God our decision to dedicate our mind to loving our Parent in everything we do.

A mind in love with God would not let itself be dominated by the material side of life or by the mind's consciousness of duty. Rather, as we are able, we exercise and develop each of the mind's three, basic, God-given capacities for practical, factual, and scientific knowledge; wisdom that comes from experience, philosophy, and superhuman sources; and the adventure of relating with God, whose spirit lives within.

To balance these three capacities means that none are omitted and none taken to excess. In each region of reality (material, intellectual, and spiritual) we are able to gain intuitive insight. Just as we may allow our positive feelings to blossom in worship, so we may seek for the mind to blossom in insightful intuition.

The example of Zacchaeus shows all these levels of mind working together. Reasoning intuitively about physical facts, he saw that the crowd in front of him was packed. Being short and realizing that he would not be able to see Jesus, he intuited that climbing up a tree would solve the problem.

When Jesus saw Zacchaeus in the tree and called him by name, there was an immediate intuitive, spiritual connection between them. He said that he would stay with him. Jesus was revealing divine mercy. When Zacchaeus insightfully realized that he had been forgiven, it triggered his spiritual rebirth.

Then Zacchaeus intuitively realized the moral significance of the injustice of getting wealthy by oppressing the poor. In response, he made his public commitment to give half his possessions to the poor and repay fourfold anyone he had cheated (Lk 19:1–10).

Loving God with all our mind, we can experience meaning and value *beginning with the smallest step forward*. We discover how *easy* it can be, how *enjoyable* it is, how *meaningful* it is to cooperate with the Creator's gifts, and *how beautifully each capacity complements the others*.

This is how our spiritual loving becomes intelligent and wise.

With all our strength

To love God fully, we mobilize all our strength for whatever our Parent has for us to do. We activate the entire personality—body, mind, and soul—to do the divine will. This mobilizing is a cooperative process, and God is the senior partner. The almighty Sovereign is the primary source of all our powers. "The Lord is my strength and my song" (Ps 118:14 RSV). "On the day I called, you answered me; you increased my strength [or boldness] of *soul*" (Ps 138:3). "Those who wait for the Lord shall renew their strength" (Is 40:31). Depending on God required Jesus to have complete faith and trust in God.

Physical strength is essential because the body both supports a mind capable of hosting the divine spirit and also enables us to act in the world. This is how love becomes real. Physical strength, flexibility, and stamina are needed if and when the battle for survival is ours to fight. Many jobs like carpentry require physical strength. And we take care of the body by healthy habits of nutrition, rest, and exercise.

We also need strength of mind, such as knowledge and wisdom. Jesus would have grasped the insight in the proverb, "Wise warriors are mightier than strong ones, and those who have knowledge than those who have [only physical] strength" (Prv 24:5, Is 11:1–4). *Receiving God's love and returning it with all our heart, soul, mind, and strength show the beauty and power of the first circuit of love.*

You Shall Love Your Neighbor as Yourself

Love wants to do good to others. As love for God fills us, it spills over into loving other persons. As we are able, we want to do good to everyone, directly or indirectly.

If we ask God, "What can I do for you?" the answer might be, "Love me, love my family. I love everyone. As you become like me, you will increasingly learn to love each person whom you have the opportunity to get to know. And remember: your love is to be intelligent and wise."

Jesus said that the commandment to love the neighbor was *like* the commandment to love God. This is true in three ways.

- Neighbor love can be called *the second circuit of love.* Since the divine spirit is also present in our neighbors, the love that we give to others also comes back to God.

- Our wholeheartedness in loving God is also expressed by doing the divine will wholeheartedly in serving our neighbors.

- God is the source of the love that we give both to our Parent and also to others.

If we identify with God's love for others, a new vista comes into view. We love not only with the love of a sibling, but also with a parental love. *We allow our Parent to live through us.*

The great challenge with the neighbor is to love persons very different from ourselves: strangers, competitors, opponents, and enemies. Jesus taught, "Love your enemies; do good to those who hate you; bless those who curse you; pray for those who mistreat you" (Lk 6:27–36, Mt 5:43–48). In the ancient Mediterranean world, the maxim of doing good to friends and harm to enemies was widespread. How often do we give generous treatment to those we like and those who are like us—motivated by the expectation or hope of being well-treated in return? When the dominant motive is self-centered, Godly love waits for another opportunity to give us (again) the taste of the joy of self-forgetting, loving service.[27]

Relevant to this topic is a student's project report. During her first project in the world religions course, this student (who wishes to remain anonymous) used Centering Prayer to cultivate her realization of God's presence within. She concluded, "I think that the biggest thing I learned from this project is that if you have the right attitude and mind, then it affects your whole being, your actions, words, feelings, etc. If you take the time to make yourself feel good and let your inner divine shine, you can make an impact on others as well."

Her second report began this way:

> It feels like everyday you hear someone say that they hate something, whether it is a class, a family member, a friend, or somebody they barely know anything about. I used to be this way as well, thinking and truly believing that I hated certain things and people. This project has made me see that hating is much worse than I thought it was; it is not something that should just be thrown around.
>
> The point of this project was to bring two things into my life. One was to love God with everything that I have and to love my neighbors as myself. I started this project pretty quickly after it was explained. I was eager to go out into the world with a new perspective and see everyone through new eyes. . . .
>
> When I started out, I thought it was going to be pretty easy, but I was wrong. At first, I was just doing the bare minimum and not applying myself. I knew that I had more effort in me, and by the end of the second week, I was putting all of my effort into it. I have learned a lot, and I have grown as a person. There were many challenges I had to overcome during this project, and some were pretty hard to face.
>
> I knew there was a deeper meaning to this project, something that I really needed to ponder. Why was it hard for me to love others? This is what I have been taught in church all of my life growing up, as well as the teaching to love God with all your heart. After a week of journaling and

reflecting, I realized that there was something about myself that I did not want to confront, but I knew I had to.

[She listed a number of things in herself that she did not like, including her body and getting poor grades on tests even though she worked hard.] I would worry that I did not love God as much as I could because I was not grateful enough for the body, mind, and soul I was made with. Whenever I wrote these ideas down in my journal and read it, I felt like I was in a sinking hole and could not get out. It was a depressing moment for me, and I was scared. I was raised never to give up, though, no matter what is standing in my path.

I decided to take a step back again and focus on the suggested golden rule, treating people how I want to be treated. . . . This time around I thought about being compassionate and putting myself in the other person's shoes. I would think about how I felt when someone did something nice for me. It makes me feel great . . . Even if it is a small gesture like a smile, it feels like they are not judging me, it makes me feel like I am not invisible.

Whenever I had this mindset, it really changed me a lot. I wanted to do these things to make people feel like they mattered, and make someone's day a little brighter.

Then something amazing happened. I felt that . . . I needed a message from God. [The next time when I went to church,] the whole mass was about loving God and loving your neighbor as the two most important commandments. I was supposed to be at that mass; the readings and the explanation of the readings from Father were my message. During that mass we talked about loving your neighbor and loving your one and only God as being two sides of the same coin. This was a great analogy, and it really got the point across to me. God is love. You cannot love God without loving your neighbor, and you cannot love your neighbor without loving God.... Whenever I thought about this, I had this great feeling of happiness and joy come over me. It almost seemed that it was bursting through my soul, almost as if I was radiating my joyous feelings. I realized that God loved me for me. God is love. God is not going to judge me for my mistakes. I am not perfect.... God made everyone in his image, so if he loves me, there is no reason why I should not love myself. It was such a great experience, and such an overwhelming amount of emotions rushed through me, it is hard to explain. It did happen, and it also changed my life.

Fortunately, it is not the only thing that changed that day.... That awesome feeling of love kept surging through me, and I felt so peaceful. [Then she was able to stop hating her ex-boyfriend who had cheated on her.]

With all these new ways of life bouncing around in my soul, mind, and heart, I feel like a much happier person. I know that I love God with everything I have. I appreciate all that he has given me, and I thank him every day. I also know that I love my neighbors as myself, and it feels great because I know I am not doing it just because it is a command. I am doing it because I owe it to God and I love God. God made everyone around me, and I should be open to at least try to love them.

Toward the end of this project I realized many things. I realized how strong of a connection one can have with God and how important it is to love your neighbors as yourself. To do all these things, you have to accept yourself for who you are. I was also lucky enough to get an amazing realization about life and God. My journey was something I will always remember, and I am proud of myself for not giving in when things were not pretty.

In sum, the first sentence of this chapter bears repeating. "Everything previously said in this book leads up to love, and everything that comes afterward flows from love." After a reflection on receiving God's love, the concepts of loving God wholeheartedly and the neighbor as oneself were introduced. We saw in detail how we can love God with all our heart, soul, mind, and strength. Then we saw how the two love commandments are alike; and a student paper illustrated much of the chapter concretely. The next two chapters portray love as accomplishing its mission to the neighbor through forgiveness and service.

Questions and Invitations

- What obstacles get in the way of receiving God's love for you? What makes it hardest for you to love God and your neighbors wholeheartedly?

- How have you succeeded in receiving and giving love when obstacles were present?

- How do you interpret Jesus's vocabulary, "heart, soul, mind, and strength"?

15

Being Merciful and Forgiving

To KNOW THAT we are truly, divinely forgiven is a transforming experience. It begins slowly and often continues gradually. We are made whole. An image of this can be found in a film, *The Green Mile*. Most of the action occurs in a prison where men who have been convicted of capital crimes and sentenced to death are awaiting execution. A friendship develops between one of the guards (played by Tom Hanks) and an enormous, magnificent, compassionate black prisoner who turns out to be innocent (played by Michael Clarke Duncan). One day, the guard was coughing and sneezing. He chanced to walk very close to the cell of this prisoner, who suddenly grabbed hold of him with both arms and held him tightly against the bars of his cell, as close as possible to his chest. Then the film showed a visualization of warm, glowing, orange light in the prisoner's chest, as he inhaled black specks of disease into his own lungs, where the specks vanished into nothing.

I personally regard this image of healing as symbolizing the work of divine mercy, motivated by love, and ultimately accomplished in the soul by the spirit of God.

Said Jesus, "Be merciful even as your Father is merciful" (Lk 6:36). This is one of the most important ways in which human beings can begin to become and be like our divine Parent. The concept of mercy is associated with tenderness, pity, kindness, compassion, and a lesser punishment than justice alone would require. I regard mercy as a divine attitude, which I equate with compassion. When I speak of forgiveness, I have in mind mercy plus the various practices that apply it in specific situations.

God's Compassion as an Overarching Divine Attitude

When the Creator chose to make imperfect beings, he smiled. He knew we were going to need mercy. We can hardly sense how far we are from the perfection to which we are invited. The good news is that our need of mercy is abundantly provided for in God's loving nature *plus his perfect understanding of us*, including complete knowledge of the pluses and minuses in ourselves and in our environment.

Mercy is essential to the practice of loving the neighbor. If divine love plus perfect understanding leads to mercy, this suggests a way for us when we find it hard to be merciful. First, we can draw more deeply on the love that is present within and use that as the lens through which to view the other person in the second circuit of love. Then we seek a greater understanding of the other person.

Jesus expressed the divine attitude of mercy at the heart of his mission when he said that he had "come to seek out and save the lost." Jesus's parable of the prodigal son teaches the way of divine compassion. A father had two sons, and the younger one asked his father to give him his inheritance early. Upon receiving it, he left home, wasted it in wild living, fell on hard times, came to his senses, and started for home. "But while he was still far off, his father saw him and was filled with compassion; he ran and put his arms around him and kissed him." The son asked to be received as one with the status of a servant; but the father brushed that idea aside, and celebrated his son's complete restoration with a great dinner (Lk 15:11–32).

The fact that the father saw him while he was still far away and was filled with compassion symbolizes the constancy of God's attitude of mercy.

The importance of restoring a person who had been lost is made clear in the last part of the parable. The older, obedient son resented the fact that a feast was being given for his younger brother. The father encouraged him to join the celebration, saying, "This brother of yours was dead and has come to life." This is equivalent to resurrection. *Coming back home to the God of mercy and returning to one's place in the family are a matter of spiritual life and death.*

How Jesus Forgave One Person's Sin

Jesus said that he had come to call not the righteous but sinners to repent. How he did this in practice was shown at another feast.

> One of the Pharisees asked Jesus to eat with him, and he went into the Pharisee's house and took his place at the table. And a woman in the city, who was a sinner, having learned

that he was eating in the Pharisee's house, brought an alabaster jar of ointment. . . . [Weeping, she] began to bathe his feet with her tears and to dry them with her hair. Then she continued kissing his feet and anointing them with the ointment. Now when the Pharisee who had invited him saw it, he said to himself, "If this man were a prophet, he would have known who and what kind of woman this is who is touching him—that she is a sinner." Jesus spoke up and said to him, "Simon, I have something to say to you." "Teacher," he replied, "speak." "A certain creditor had two debtors; one owed five hundred denarii, and the other fifty. When they could not pay, he canceled the debts for both of them. Now which of them will love him more?" Simon answered, "I suppose the one for whom he canceled the greater debt." And Jesus said to him, "You have judged rightly." Then turning toward the woman, he said to Simon, "Do you see this woman? I entered your house; you gave me no water for my feet, but she has bathed my feet with her tears and dried them with her hair. You gave me no kiss, but from the time I came in she has not stopped kissing my feet. You did not anoint my head with oil, but she has anointed my feet with ointment. Therefore, I tell you, her sins, which were many, have been forgiven; hence she has shown great love. But the one to whom little is forgiven, loves little." Then he said to her, "Your sins are forgiven." But those who were at the table with him began to say among themselves, "Who is this who even forgives sins?" And he said to the woman, "Your faith has saved you; go in peace" (Lk 7:36–50).

It is plausible that the woman had been part of a crowd who had seen Jesus; she had heard his message and realized that his words of love, mercy, assurance, and hope were also meant for her, too. Transformed by faith, she came into this house (in accord with the custom) where a meal for several people was being given. She boldly expressed her gratitude and love.

Before Jesus sent her forth in peace, he made it clear that her sins had been forgiven, and that her faith had saved her—in the sense that her receptive-and-active faith was essential to completing the work of divine mercy. Jesus's assurance also suggests another lesson. Once we truly know that we are forgiven, our work is to sustain faith in the mercy that we have received. It is easy to feel that some sort of lingering odor clings to the self, like an inescapable stain. But no matter how others may regard us, living faith strides forward in security and confidence. When divine forgiveness is truly received in the soul, a new sense of self is born. To be a daughter or son of God now gains more meaning and value. I believe that this forgiven woman also experienced in her heart that Jesus's loving forgiveness had destroyed her sin. In addition, the salvation that she had received by faith restored her strength, so that she could start fresh in the new and better way of living.

In this episode, critics of Jesus correctly pointed out that to forgive sins is to act in the name of God. Jesus spoke with authority and managed the situation in the power of God. It is striking that Jesus called us to be like he was—merciful as God is merciful. Mercy can be part of our daily attitude toward people. *It activates the truth that we are all siblings.*

Forgiving and Reconciliation

Jesus clearly implied the need to forgive others first before seeking forgiveness from God. He taught us to pray, "Forgive us our debts as we also have forgiven our debtors" (Mt 6:12).

A friend had been turning over in his mind how his wife had hurt him. He came into the living room and saw her bending over her knitting. As a blanketeer, she was creating another small, artistic blanket for some child she would never see. As soon as he saw her, he had a vision of divine mercy coming down from heaven, surrounding her like a great silo of compassionate light. Then, in utter amazement, he wandered aimlessly into the kitchen, in awe of the mercy that he had just seen embracing her. The thought came to him: this same mercy must be available to him, too! And immediately he was surrounded with an identical silo of light—and felt completely free.

Just as we need to respond with forgiveness to those who mistreat us, we equally need, with those we have harmed, to make things right as we are able. Jesus did not say, "Forgive yourself." He said, "When you are offering your gift at the altar, if you remember that your brother or sister has something against you, leave your gift there before the altar and go; first be reconciled to your brother or sister, and then come and offer your gift" (Mt 5:23–24). Only then, Jesus implied, can we worship "in spirit and in truth" (Jn 4:24).

Repenting may include many steps

Before getting into the topic of repentance, it is important to clear up a common confusion. Some persons struggle with oppressive guilt feelings and need to distinguish two kinds of guilt. Real guilt is the awareness of having violated the divine way. False guilt can arise when one has gone against social expectations that do not reflect what is truly right and wrong. Or we may have fallen short of our own ideal, but not short of the will of the realistic and compassionate God.

But after doing bad things, some people confess with their lips but do nothing to change. For repentance, the change of mind, to become real, it may involve a number of things.

- Reflect morally to sharpen our understanding about what we did
- Get factually clear about what chain of events led up to the problem behavior, with what consequences, and how we could have acted differently at each step along the way
- Be reconciled with the person we have wronged; make things right as we are able
- Apologize to the Father of the infinitely loved child we have harmed
- Receive divine forgiveness in faith

Upon the "dust and ashes" of our repentance falls a promise: "You shall be like a watered garden" (Job 42:6, Is 58:11).

A Community Process of Forgiveness

It is common to hear people recommend forgiveness because it frees the one who forgives from being torn up by negative attitudes. This fact is gloriously true, and it can take a lot of work to get that far. But in addition to these genuine and important benefits, the forgiveness that Jesus taught may also require the person who is forgiving to interact with the wrongdoer, if it is reasonably possible to do so. Sometimes this process requires more than one person.

The Master gave instructions for a grievance procedure for a community of believers that begins with one-to-one mercy and may terminate in justice as determined by the group (Mt 18:12–34). He introduced it with the parable of the lost sheep. It begins like this. "Which one of you, having a hundred sheep and losing one of them, does not leave the ninety-nine in the wilderness and go after the one that is lost until he finds it? When he has found it, he lays it on his shoulders and rejoices." The fact that the shepherd goes out to find the sheep that has gone astray has a clear implication in this context. The parable implies that *the purpose of the forgiveness procedure that follows is to bring a lost soul back into the circuits of loving community.*

To accomplish this, three steps may be needed.

1. Jesus said that if someone sins against you (in the sense of serious, deliberate wrongdoing), go to that person one-to-one, and establish a shared understanding of what went wrong. If the wrongdoer refuses to cooperate, move to the next step.

2. Go to the person a second time, taking one or two others who can give evidence to confirm the fact of wrongdoing, especially if the problem continues.

3. If the wrongdoer still refuses to acknowledge what he or she has done and persists in the harmful behavior, then the whole group can gather to hear the dispute. The group may decide to stop welcoming that person in their gatherings.

Thinking of stage three, it is easy to imagine oneself looking down on a person who is on trial. To correct a judgmental attitude,

Jesus first clarified that one needs to be prepared to forgive many, many times. It can take a long time for a wrongdoer to replace bad habits and triumph over evil tendencies. One who is struggling to grow needs others to be patient, kind, and supportive.

Then Jesus told another parable. A person was forgiven a huge debt by his superior, but this forgiven man threw into prison someone who owed him a very small debt but could not pay. When the superior heard what the forgiven man had done, he punished him severely. This parable reminds us of how great the salvation is that we have received by being mercifully welcomed into the family of God, no matter how serious our previous wrongdoing may have been.

One reason why this three-step procedure is not done more often is that many people who recognize the harm caused by a judgmental attitude do not understand that there are some kinds of judgments that we need to make as responsible members of society. Some believers quote Jesus's teaching, "Do not judge," out of context. Consider.

> Do not judge, so that you may not be judged. For the judgment you give will be the judgment you get, and the measure you give will be the measure you get. Why do you see the speck in your neighbor's eye but do not notice the log in your own eye? Or how can you say to your neighbor, "Let me take the speck out of your eye," while the log is in your own eye? You hypocrite, first take the log out of your own eye, and then you will see clearly to take the speck out of your neighbor's eye. Do not give what is holy to dogs, and do not throw your pearls before swine, or they will trample them under foot and turn and maul you (Mt 7:1–6).

By combining these teachings, Jesus prompted his listeners to draw a distinction: judging souls is none of our business. But one of our responsibilities is to judge wisely, recognizing the danger posed by some persons in society.

Should a community enforce basic standards when they are violated or allow itself to be torn apart? This is what Jesus is giving guidance about. This is an example of the need for practical realism to complement spiritual idealism.

Considering the two parables and the three-stage procedure, we observe that mercy is applied to the individual with due regard for justice and community welfare, the long-term good of the whole.

Clearly, step one, a conversation in private, sometimes called a 'carefrontation,' has a lot of advantages over angry reacting. Conversations in step two are surprisingly powerful; most people entering a group would profit from training in this procedure. I have seen groups benefit from sessions on each of the three steps, exploring why Jesus's grievance procedure seems so hard to work with, and how to adapt it to their particular situation.

Without love, mercy decays into an attitude of looking down upon the other person. Without understanding, love is diffuse and less helpful. The practices of forgiveness, reconciliation, and rehabilitation powerfully uphold one-to-one relationships and groups.

Summary and Transition

We hear some people speak of mercy as though it immediately sweeps everything away and lets us off scot-free. There is no judgment to face; we will never be held accountable; we have no work of repentance to do as a member of a community.

By contrast, Jesus's teachings give us the height and depth of pervading, transforming mercy. And the Master also made it clear that we need to repent in socially responsible ways, and wisely forgive others, too.

Mercy is the first application of Godly love to the adventure of loving the neighbor. In my opinion, the attitude of mercy and the outworking of forgiveness are already contained implicitly in God's love. Mercy is a constant, overarching divine attitude that we are called to participate in. We are to be merciful as God is merciful. Also like the prodigal son, our need for mercy can be a matter of spiritual life and death. As recipients of mercy, we need to cooperate with the understanding compassion that is reaching out to us. This cooperation may include our personal process of repenting, which may involve many steps of growth.

The steps of the community process that Jesus taught are designed to lead the wrongdoer back into the circuits of loving community and to protect the community. We who are beginners in these things may have no experience of a community dedicated to these practices. Realism does not expect of ourselves too much, too fast, as we learn new ways. But when we approach people in an attitude of friendship, our work of understanding compassion, forgiveness, reconciliation, and carefrontation has the best chance to succeed.

The next application of divine love is service, which goes into action by doing good to others. We now realize that service that is truly loving is also merciful. Mercy brings the eyes of compassionate understanding to the question of how best to serve others. Doing good brings a fitting completion to love's applications with the neighbor. The next chapter shows three types of Jesus's service.

Questions and Invitations

- How can you identify with God's overarching attitude of mercy when you recall Jesus saying that we should be merciful as God is merciful?

- What obstacles keep you from implementing one or more of the community grievance procedures that Jesus taught? Consider using carefrontation to help another person understand what happened, and why it was wrong, even as you support the person in their growth process.

- Who has forgiven you in a way that you found compassionate and constructive?

16

Doing Good to Others

FOR SEVERAL YEARS, I worked with an evangelistic group in Berkeley, California, that numbered over forty volunteers. One woman who joined the group, Susan Shupp, got a job working in Oakland Children's Hospital. Her assignment was to love infants who were so deprived of affectionate attention that they were in serious condition. To love them, she would hold each one, touch them and gently move their hands and legs; and coo, speak, and sing cheerfully for forty-five minutes. Soon, she found herself exhausted at the end of each day. Then one morning, she said, "OK, Father. You love them through me." That day she went through her whole workday sustaining good energy. During the remaining months that she stayed in that job, she used the same approach every day and got the same results. She spoke of this experience without a trace of self-importance; and she radiated the joy of service.

She had entered into Jesus's way of selfless service. She was motivated by the love that comes from God; and she had a compassionate understanding of the needs of those she served. Her warm smile and laughing heart poured out love in an easy, gentle, natural way. Jesus described himself and his mission in terms of service. "I am among you as one who serves"; "the Son of Man did not come to be served, but to serve" (Lk 22:27, Mk 10:45).

Love wants to do good to people, and service actually does so. The importance of *doing* in the spiritual life is emphasized in Jesus's parable that begins: "Everyone who hears these words of mine and does them will be like a wise man who built his house on the rock" (Mt 7:24).

This chapter highlights three aspects of Jesus's loving service: social service, especially healing; teaching, especially the golden rule; and evangelism—interacting with others and giving voice to gospel truth. Each section presents some challenging standards and some ideas for gradually approaching them.

We also approach the more demanding types of service by deepening our acquaintance with the foundations for service presented in the two previous chapters. We reenter the first circuit of love—receive God's love for us as we are able and love our Parent in return with our heart, soul, mind, and strength. Then, in the second circuit of love, we practice loving the neighbor with the overarching attitude of mercy and recommit to reconciliation and forgiveness. On this dual basis, our loving and compassionate service can grow without limits.

Social Service

Collectively speaking, individuals and organizations dedicated to social service offer help to persons with the full spectrum of human problems. Familiar examples include working in a soup kitchen or participating in a Habitat for Humanity team that builds houses for people who cannot afford one.

Much loving service is low-key: smiles, friendly greetings, and holding the door open for someone; the next level is checking in on others, which takes time and might involve us in doing more. Jesus called us to all kinds of service, and his life demonstrated that we can be about God's business in one way or another every day.

Going to great lengths in selfless service is sometimes called going "the second mile." In Jesus's day, a Jewish man might be legally forced by a Roman soldier to carry his pack for one mile. An unarmed man who was pressed into service could fight the soldier or obey passively. But Jesus wanted us to be active in responding with good to whatever evil comes our way. Imagine how the soldier might be affected if the Jewish brother were to carry his pack for a second mile. What quality of silence may they have experienced, what quality of conversation, what bonding by the end of the second mile?

In my opinion, the greatest example of social service in Jesus's teachings is the good Samaritan. Jesus told this parable in discussion with an expert in religious law who intended to challenge the Master. But the expert ended up confessing that the way to eternal life is to love God and the neighbor. A bit later, the lawyer asked defensively, "Who is my neighbor?" This was Jesus's reply:

> A man was going down from Jerusalem to Jericho, and fell into the hands of robbers, who stripped him, beat him, and went away, leaving him half dead. Now by chance a priest was going down that road; and when he saw him, he passed by on the other side. So likewise a Levite, when he came to the place and saw him, passed by

on the other side. But a Samaritan while traveling came near him; and when he saw him, he was moved with pity. He went to him and bandaged his wounds, having poured oil and wine on them. Then he put him on his own animal, brought him to an inn, and took care of him. The next day he took out two denarii and said, "Take care of him; and when I come back, I will repay you whatever more you spend." Which of these three, do you think, was a neighbor to the man who fell into the hands of the robbers?" He said, "The one who showed him mercy." Jesus said to him, "Go and do likewise" (Lk 10:25–37).

Jesus told this parable to challenge the centuries-long prejudice of many Jews toward Samaritans, who had a long history of antagonism toward Jews. The parable shows that an outstanding example of ministry can be found in a person in the family of faith who is not part of our own religious group. The parable also portrays the potential practical implications of neighbor love. This example of healing took time, skill, strength, money, and responsibility after the initial effort. The Samaritan exhibits a character of righteousness in perfect maturity.

During his last few years on earth, Jesus was mainly focused on leading the gospel movement that he had started. But service was part of the message. Jesus's most common form of social service was healing. He was filled with compassion, and his healing power flowed forth on many occasions.

Jesus called his apostles and evangelists to heal the sick, and they did so sometimes with deeds of power. But it is also plausible that they also often ministered to the sick in natural and ordinary ways, giving support for their faith as they regained health and wellness in body, mind, and soul. We all have some capacity to do both kinds of healing; and it is our privilege to develop our potentials of prayer and service from whatever level we presently find ourselves.

I am not a healer, though I hope that my efforts in conversation will do some good. When we pray for someone in need of healing, we can pray for the person's mind to be completely filled with faith in order to facilitate the work of divine spirit. In addition, we can turn and plunge into focusing on God. Then, sustaining this focus, we hold the other person in mind and move into expectant silence. We start with no idea of what God may do or choose not to do, but we may receive an assurance about what will happen sooner or later.

No matter how much of a beginner we may be in these things, we can trust that our current knowledge, wisdom, and living faith empower us to do what God may ask of us now. We can learn to participate at some level in Jesus's way of healing. What happens may surprise us.

The Golden Rule

Jesus also served by teaching. One of his best-known maxims teaches us how to serve. This is the universal principle of service, the golden rule. "Do to others as you want others to do to you" (Lk 6:31, Mt 7:12). This is a rule that gives guidance on how to put neighbor love into practice and applies to all kinds of activities. It is simply stated and intuitively understandable, something that any person can work with and grow with.

I think that the golden rule is a living truth. If we work with it earnestly, we discover new meaning in it. Here are some interpretations that can be arranged in five levels of meaning.

First, treat others with consideration for their feelings, as you want others to be considerate of your feelings. Ideally, we learn the practice of the golden rule early in life. Practice cultivates empathy; we learn to imagine ourselves in the place of the other. And we can normally expect family and friends to reciprocate for the good we do by treating us in a kindly manner.

But the golden rule is not restricted, for example, to empathy, consideration, and sympathy. It implies more than this, which leads to the next level, since the family is part of a wider culture.

Second, treat others in your culture in accord with established norms, as you want others to do to you. This might mean entering into the spirit and practices of popular holidays, such as Christmas. In some cultures the golden rule functions as a summary principle that symbolizes the tradition's moral and ethical standards. For example, Jesus spoke of the golden rule as expressing the spirit of Biblical teaching (Mt 7:12). But cultures are diverse, and the rule obliges us to adjust for the other person's tradition, such as Hanukkah. Thus, the rule moves us beyond only being respectful of the habits of one's own culture.

Third, treat others in accord with moral reason, as you want others to do to you. The golden rule, in and of itself, does not give any specific advice for particular situations. Its generality is not attached to any one culture. It is found in many cultures; in one form or another, it is the most universal moral maxim on the planet. This makes it applicable in every relationship in every situation everywhere. The practice of the rule cultivates recognition of, and respect for, universal humanity.

Fourth, treat others as siblings, children of God, as you want others to treat you. This spiritual level is the golden rule as *the principle of the practice of the family of God*.

But in the universal family not everyone is going to reciprocate our kindness, respect our cultural norms, or cherish any principles of moral reason. This fact calls for another spiritual level.

Fifth, treat others in accord with God-like love, as you want others to treat you. As Jesus commanded his followers, "Love one another as I have loved you" (Jn 13:34). In Jesus's love are resources to deal with all the limitations of lower-level interpretations of the rule.

For example, in Luke, the golden rule is placed in the middle of Jesus's lesson on loving our enemies (Lk 6:27–36, Mt 5:38–48). This context clearly implies that followers of Jesus are expected to return good for evil. The idea of enemies can be generalized to a wide range of people who are difficult to deal with, for example, greedy people who abuse their economic power, and antagonistic opponents in society and all levels of politics from local to global. We cannot expect all these persons to do reciprocal good in return for any service that we do for them. Here the golden rule tests our motivation: do we do good only because we expect or hope for benefits in return? Then our motive is self-centered, which is not the way of the golden rule.[28]

In context, Jesus's command to love as he loved us calls us to be willing to lay down our life for others. It is worthwhile considering how we may prepare ourselves for such a challenge. We can, over the years, prepare ourselves for this kind of test by making decisions in advance about what we would do if we were in a situation that might call for putting our life on the line. Some people do this as part of their vocation, such as soldiers; and some persons because of their religion are at risk in their community. At least we can form pre-made decisions for imagined situations. For example, if I catch myself indulging in some unbeautiful attitude toward someone, I can say: I would lay down my life—if it were the will of God (I imagine praying three times to make sure)—to defend persons like this one if they are attacked.

For most people, most of the time, the practice of the golden rule takes place in socially supportive situations and involves being responsible parents, students, workers, and good citizens generally. This rule will one day prevail among humankind, and our privilege is to live the golden rule in a manner that foreshadows, consistent with factual realism, a better world.

A person who chooses to grow with this rule might consider these questions. How would I respond to the rule if I heard the Master directly tell it to me? How have I been well treated by others in the past? If I were in the other person's place, would I like to be treated in the same way that I'm getting ready to treat this person? What advice would Jesus give regarding the same type of situation that I'm in now? What would Jesus do?

Giving Voice to the Gospel

Evangelism is a category of social service and an application of the golden rule. If I were one of the lost, how would I want to be treated by a God-knowing person who sensed my condition? I would want this person to help me find true and real life. And believers, including evangelists, sometimes get lost.

For Jesus, proclaiming the message was an expression of love, wanting the world to know the joys of an abundant life in God. The message was front and center in his mission, his highest expression of service: "Let us go on to the neighboring towns, so that I may proclaim the message there also; for that is what I came out to do" (Mk 1:38).

To proclaim means to make something known by announcing it publicly. Jesus taught in synagogues, in the Jerusalem Temple, and to whoever showed up in the many towns and villages where he traveled with the twelve.

Authentic proclaiming is based on living the truths of Jesus's message as we are able. *Jesus proclaimed most of all by his life.*

And the religion that he lived was the religion that he taught. A person who is fully committed to the mission of the gospel, active even on a very part-time basis, can find in Jesus a new strength of conviction and a moving sincerity in relation with the other. Thus, the messenger is enabled to speak with added power—not the material force of threats and fury, but the spiritual power of love, mercy, and service.[29]

Guidance for gospel messengers can be found in Jesus's parable of the sower.

> Listen! A sower went out to sow. And as he sowed, some seeds fell on the path, and the birds came and ate them up. Other seeds fell on rocky ground, where they did not have much soil, and they sprang up quickly, since they had no depth of soil. But when the sun rose, they were scorched; and since they had no root, they withered away. Other seeds fell among thorns, and the thorns grew up and choked them. Other seeds fell on good soil and brought forth grain, some a hundredfold, some sixty, some thirty. Let anyone with ears to hear listen! (Mt 13:1–23).

The last line, telling those with ears to hear listen, encourages us to persevere. Those of us who aspire to "bring forth a lot of grain" should understand that it is normal for all of us who begin the path of faith to run into serious difficulties.

Jesus proclaimed the powerful truths of the saving message that we are exploring; and he called the twelve apostles and then seventy evangelists to reach more people. I believe that the Master intended for all his followers to participate actively in this movement. If I am right, then Jesus may be sitting across the table, smiling as he waits for us to take a good stiff drink of orange juice and get started, giving voice to gospel truths as best we can. We will get better through experience, especially when combined with study and fellowship with others who are involved in this work.

Many people are put off by evangelism for various reasons. But given its importance, we might take another look. Sometimes we face a task that we know are resisting, but we push ourselves out of our comfort zone and get started, which is often enough to generate an appetite for more. But is there a way of expanding our comfort zone first? I believe there is. Some people find it helpful to begin by living the truth and proclaiming *silently*. This includes to

- Pray at length, say, thirty minutes, for the other person
- Ponder what truths of the gospel speak to the person's need
- Imagine expressing that truth by what you could say and do
- Consider what questions one might use to begin a conversation
- Pray for an opportunity to do so

These silent, inner activities are indeed part of living the gospel. Such activities make a big difference, and they become even more effective when we begin to be taken in hand by that greatest of teachers—experience.

A next step is to find uplifting responses in everyday situations. For example, in response to "How are you?," I have often used, "Glad to see you," or "Better because of you." One of my favorite answers worked wonders in a parking lot. It was the end of the workday, and an acquaintance whose car was ten yards away asked me, "How are you?" "Joyous and grateful," I replied. Months later we ran into each other in the student center, and she told me that my simple reply had had a major effect on her. She had been irritable and complaining, and suddenly decided to change her habitual attitudes—and succeeded.

To be consistent with the golden rule, giving voice to gospel truth does not dispense a packaged, one-size-fits-all message to strangers and then walk away. In one-to-one situations, we may begin with socializing, for example, by noticing and asking about something about the other person. Then comes getting to know something about the other person—and sharing personally about oneself. When the relationship has begun to be real, the other person may become receptive to our sharing of what has become meaningful in our own experience.

As I noted above, going door-to-door is a different kind of activity. We can say, "I'm your neighbor, [name], encouraging you in the faith that you are a [son or daughter] of God." Then fall silent with a smile and let the conversation go from there. A sense of humor helps. I was knocking and could hear music playing inside, but no one opened the door—until I started knocking to the beat of the music. It was a genuinely spiritual and delightfully fun conversation. And there are countless additional approaches. Anyone with the supreme desire to share the gospel will find ways to do so.

Proclaiming the gospel is not the same as telling people about what Jesus said and commenting on it. The great teachers and prophets were not content to quote and comment; this is more along the lines of what some scribes and rabbis did (Mt 7:29). Rather, we are to give fresh expression to the truth of the message in the light of our own experience and our unique way of putting it.

One of the best evangelists I have ever known would delight in meeting people of all kinds. Ed Owen had been homeless for years, and he knew how to get along with all types of people. With a broad and warm smile, he met people in love and kindness; his conversation was relaxed and easy. He would ask questions and listen. He said very little in the way of spiritual teaching; he would often give a taste of joy and liberty with just a single sentence, or a question. But what he did say was a genuinely meaningful thought that could stay in the other person's heart and mind; many times he found out later that his brief words had a considerable impact. He was completely at peace with giving a simple, gentle nudge. (His nudges on the manuscript of this book greatly improved it.) When asked what his religion was, he would always say, "I am a son of God, and I am your brother."

Summary and Transition

Jesus proclaimed his message above all by a life in which love and mercy motivated and guided his ministry. It is natural for us to be challenged by his high ideals for us, which include second-miler social service, becoming active in the gospel movement, faith healing, and living in a way that is prepared to stake one's life. But there are steps of gradual approach to these goals, plus our constant divine support.

This chapter culminates the unfolding of love through compassion and service to the neighbor. Part III is around the corner, and chapter 17 narrates what leads up to and what is the great pivot in Jesus's gospel message.

Questions and Invitations

- How can you best support others in gaining health and wellness? And how might you add to your skills?

- Consider these questions from this chapter. How would I respond to the golden rule if I heard the Master directly tell it to me? How have I been well treated by others in the past? Would I like to be treated in the same way that I'm getting ready to treat this person? What advice would Jesus give regarding the same type of situation that I'm in? What would Jesus do?

- In what ways do you give voice to gospel truths? How could love, mercy, and practice expand your comfort zone in proclaiming?

Part III
THE SON OF GOD REVEALS HIS DIVINITY

Now we enter the narrative of the momentous actions of the Master as he managed the conflict between himself and some of the religious leaders. His life was at stake, and so was their salvation. This was a trying time for Jesus, and also for his apostles and disciples who had important lessons to learn from how he handled harassment, crisis, and persecution.

Jesus launched the third stage of his life in accord with his Father's will: he responded to his enemies, first, by proclaiming his advanced gospel teachings. To his original message he added truths centered on his divinity as the Son of God. The combination of basic and advanced teachings was the full gospel, which was still centered in the fatherhood of God and the brotherhood of man.

Now we see Jesus stay loyal to the Father's will through his most difficult times. As his followers today, we can learn much from how Jesus handled these situations as the Good Shepherd revealing the truth in love.

As spirit-taught knowers of gospel truth, we are tested on the way to becoming spirit-led. We all have burdens to bear, a cross that is ours to pick up. As we follow Jesus, we aim to do things that work toward the short- and long-term good of everyone affected.

17
Responding to Different Levels of Hostility

IMAGINE HOW A rapidly spreading religious movement would attract the attention of local religious authorities in the ancient world, as it would attract attention now. In the densely populated region of southern Galilee, the Son of Man was well received by many people. He gathered and trained the twelve apostles, and later sent forth seventy evangelists. The message of the kingdom and family of God spread quickly.

Occasionally, seemingly minor conflicts with his enemies came to the surface. But then came the major clash—the turning point. This heated opposition gathered in Capernaum, on the northwestern shore of the Sea of Galilee, which had served for a time as the headquarters for Jesus and the apostles.

This chapter probes six events that led up to, and came to a head in, what we read in John 6: three brief episodes; two dramatic actions (Jesus's feeding the five thousand and his refusal to be made king); and the great and pivotal clash in Jesus's public ministry.

Why Some Religious Leaders Felt Threatened by Jesus

After Jesus started going forth with the apostles to proclaim his message, it did not take long before they began to meet with resistance from some religious leaders. These leaders opposed him for several reasons. The first was Jesus's overall approach to religion. His freedom from conformity to the full details of the written and oral law appealed to the crowds in its liberating simplicity. Jesus built upon tradition in a way that largely ignored the religious authorities and the rituals of the Jerusalem Temple. He did not teach like scribes, the experts in the Hebrew Bible (Mt 7:29). One of their main ways of teaching was to comment, especially on portions of the first five books of the Bible that were attributed to Moses. By contrast, Jesus spoke as if he had authority in himself that came straight from God. And his teaching was centered on God, truth, and life.

And then there were healings and other wonders. The news of these traveled fast, attracting people with a variety of motivations. Jesus was doing things that the religious leaders could not compete with. His movement was beyond what they could control.

Three Brief Clashes

The three seemingly minor conflicts introduce key components of Jesus's response to hostility. One factor in two of them is that Jesus and the apostles were free from extremes in observing the

Sabbath. These episodes led to growing antagonism from the religious authorities.

One Sabbath, Jesus's disciples were plucking and rubbing the grain that was left for people to eat along the borders of a field. Some Pharisees asked Jesus why he allowed his disciples to break the law against doing any work on the Sabbath. Jesus replied, "Have you never read what David did when he and his companions were hungry and in need of food? He entered the house of God, and ate the bread of the Presence, which it is not lawful for any but the priests to eat, and he gave some to his companions."

Jesus challenged the Pharisees for going to extremes in sabbath observance. "The sabbath was made for humankind, and not humankind for the sabbath." And he concluded, "The Son of Man is lord even of the sabbath" (Mk 2:23–28, Lv 23:22, 1 Sm 22:20). Jesus revealed more about who he was in a way that was strong and final on that occasion, and he did so without any counterattacking. His reply also showed his understanding of the purpose of the Sabbath. Jesus thus revealed more of what pleases God and more of what it means to be faithful children of God.

On another Sabbath day, Jesus entered a synagogue where some Pharisees were watching to see whether he would cure a man who had a withered hand. Jesus told the man to come forward. The Pharisees interpreted healing as work, which is forbidden on the Sabbath; but Jesus reminded them of the common practice of doing various good things on the Sabbath. "Suppose one of you has only one sheep and it falls into a pit on the Sabbath; will you not lay hold of it and lift it out? How much more valuable is a human being than a sheep?" The Pharisees were silent. Jesus concluded, "So it is lawful to do good on the Sabbath." He said to the man, "Stretch out your hand." He stretched it out, and his hand was restored (Mk 3:1–5).

In this second clash, free of fear, Jesus had the presence of mind to make an insightful comparison: people would do good on the Sabbath in a similar situation of caring for a sheep. Next, he reminded his hearers of the common-sense difference in value between a human being and a sheep. Finally, he brought his reasoning to its conclusion: it is lawful to do good on the Sabbath. On this occasion, Jesus used the same kind of reasoning that the Pharisees would understand; the rabbis were trained in it. Refuted and embarrassed, in defensiveness bordering on panic, these Pharisees immediately went out and conspired with others about how to destroy Jesus (Mk 3:6). The initial interaction led his opponents to plan his murder.

On the third occasion, a paralytic who could not walk sought healing, so his friends brought him to Jesus (Mk 2:1–12). But so many people crowded around Jesus that he could not gain access. His friends took him up on the roof, opened a hole in it, and lowered him down on his mat so that he came to rest on the floor, right in front of Jesus. Observing this bold, imaginative initiative, Jesus was impressed by his faith and said, "My son, your sins are forgiven." But some of the scribes criticized Jesus in their hearts for blasphemy, because only God can forgive sins. Here the conflict is not even voiced aloud by these scribes, but it is just as real and significant either way.

Jesus knew what they were thinking and said, "Why do you raise such questions in your hearts? Which is easier, to say to the paralytic, 'Your sins are forgiven,' or to say, 'Stand up and take your mat and walk'? But so that you may know that *the Son of Man has authority on earth to forgive sins*, [he looked at the man and said,] 'I say to you, stand up, take your mat and go to your home.'" And the man did just that. Jesus did not shy away from conflict; he used it to reveal more about himself.

Feeding the Five Thousand and Then Refusing to Be Made King

There were two more dramatic events that led up to the major turning point in Jesus's ministry. After laboring in teaching and healing, Jesus and the apostles sought rest from the crowds and went off to a deserted place by themselves. The crowds pursued them insistently; but after they had been with Jesus for three days, their food supply run out. When it was late in the day, the apostles urged Jesus to send the people away to the villages to buy food for themselves. But Jesus was filled with compassion for these hungry ones, who were *"like sheep without a shepherd"* (Mk 6:34). Sheep rely on the shepherd to bring them to places where they can eat. With no shepherd, sheep are lost and vulnerable. For reasons that he did not explain, on this occasion Jesus, the Good Shepherd, chose to use his divine power. He took two fish and five barley loaves, multiplied them miraculously, and fed five thousand or more people (Jn 6:1–14).

Since the beginning of his ministry, this was the most stunning act in which Jesus's compassion and power seemed to encourage the popular hope for a wonder-working, material Messiah. The people who had been fed appear to have responded with a united wave of enthusiasm, and they were intending to seize him and make him their king. But Jesus refused and withdrew (Jn 6:15).

This first of these two events would raise expectations about Jesus as Messiah. The second would alarm the political authorities as well as the religious ones. More than ever, the question intensified. What would Jesus do next?

The Master went into the hills to pray.

The Turning Point at Capernaum

The stage was now completely set for the pivotal clash at Capernaum, much of it in the synagogue. Jesus was speaking to an audience with at least three groups: the apostles; other followers including some who had been fed with the five thousand; and enemies.

Jesus first challenged the motivation of those who had followed him to the synagogue because they had gotten free food. In contrast, he spoke of spiritual food, which "the Son of Man will give you." Then one of his assembled enemies interrupted with an insincere question to put Jesus to the test. "What sign are you going to give us then, so that we may see it and believe you? Our ancestors ate the manna in the wilderness; as it is written, "[Moses] gave them bread from heaven to eat" (Jn 6:25–31).

Jesus replied with a huge challenge and an even greater gift. "Very truly I tell you, it was not Moses who gave you the bread from heaven, but *it is my Father who gives you the true bread from heaven. For the bread of God is that which comes down from heaven and gives life to the world. . . . I am the bread of life.*" Surrounding these words, Jesus was making it abundantly clear that he was speaking of eternal life (Jn 6:27–58).

Now Jesus was calling into question the Biblical record about Moses and manna or how the scripture had been generally interpreted. But more importantly, Jesus had now proclaimed himself as having come down from heaven. And he not only offered to *give* to all the bread of life. He also revealed that he *is* the bread of life. This symbol called hearers to find ways of nourishing themselves on the bread that he is. Jesus was inviting everyone present to do so right then and there. At the very least, this would have involved accepting and welcoming him into their hearts, receiving his teachings into their minds and souls, and allowing and cooperating with the resulting transformation. And he was offering this bread of life not only to those present but also to the whole world.

Discussion and debates followed, first among the hearers who were not followers of Jesus and then among Jesus's own followers (Jn 6:52–71). He gave abundant and clear assurance that the life that he brought from heaven is eternal life; those who believe in him will live forever. In other words, Jesus, whose parents were known to some of his listeners, was not only human, but also divine. He had come down from heaven.

The events of John 6 are the turning point in the public ministry of Jesus because of several new features.

- Counterattack: first, in the challenge to those who wanted a Messiah mainly for material reasons; for example, as a source of free food

- Counterattack: next, in the challenge to scriptural tradition or its interpretation about Moses giving people manna, the bread of heaven

- The clear and public shift into *advanced teachings* which those present were hearing for the first time—*Jesus had come down from heaven; those who believe in him will live forever; and he is the bread of life, eternal life, which he offers to the world*

- The debates that followed

- The fact that, after this turning point, many of Jesus's disciples turned away and stopped following him

It had been easier to follow Jesus until a gaping rift appeared between tradition and the new religion in its fullness. Many former disciples were unwilling to go against their leaders and leave traditional security behind them.

Open hostilities had broken out at a new level. It is plausible that, soon after this, the Temple rulers began the practice of throwing believers in Jesus out of the synagogue (Jn 9:22, 12:42, 16:2).

Lessons for Us

Looking back on these early conflicts, we observe some of Jesus's qualities as a leader. They are also appropriate for us when others challenge our beliefs. Jesus responded to his critics in a manner that was *immediate, spontaneous, strong, clear, positive, limited,* and *spiritual*. He showed the calm dignity of one who was completely secure in God. When attacked, we can respond intuitively then and there. We need not retreat to prepare a response for later. The spirit of God will help us to speak clearly, with assurance, and briefly—perhaps with a note of joyful proclaiming.

Next, reviewing the clash in the Capernaum synagogue, we see new qualities in Jesus's leadership. He seemed to take the initiative in response to the opposition that had gathered. There is no duty of politeness to allow one's enemies to select the place, time, and manner of their attack. Jesus began publicly to proclaim the advanced component of the full gospel, the cluster of teachings that will center around his being the Son of God.

We have reviewed motivations for some religious leaders to resist Jesus: three brief clashes; two dramatic actions—feeding the five thousand and the king-making episode; plus the pivotal turning point at Capernaum and lessons for us today. We have also brought forth a handful of advanced teachings.

The next chapter adds to the list of advanced teachings centered on Jesus as the Son of God. It also considers their significance and how to integrate them coherently with the original message.

Questions and Invitations

- As an actual or potential leader, what lessons do you take from how Jesus managed conflict in the brief clashes and at Capernaum?

- If someone attacks you verbally, what are your options?

- How could we foster a society of non-violent communication where opponents achieve mutual understanding by listening to and voicing each other's view so that they both feel genuinely understood?[30]

18

The Advanced Level of Jesus's Gospel

THIS CHAPTER IS crucial to my concept of the gospel.

When we learn good news, nothing is more natural than to tell others—lots of others. We may be good at keeping secrets, but when the desire to share wonderful news about Jesus is bursting in our heart, it is understandable that enthusiasm might overpower wisdom.

Although Jesus revealed it mainly during the last phase of his ministry, others knew about the news. It had been communicated to Mary before Jesus's birth. It is clear that the Father wanted some people to know that his Son had come. At his baptism, the Father's voice was heard: "This is my beloved Son in whom I am well pleased" (Mt 3:17). John the Baptist was one of those who heard the voice, and he proclaimed Jesus as having come down from heaven. There would be a later occasion when the Father spoke audibly to a few. "This is my beloved Son. Listen to him" (Mt 17:5). And the Master told the Samaritan woman at the well that he was the Messiah (Jn 4:26).

But Jesus's *gospel, his good news, was his public message to the crowds.* His original message was laying an extensive and strong foundation for peoples' later reception of higher truth that Jesus was the Son of God. The sower was sowing, and much seed was sprouting. Given more time, continuing growth would naturally have led many believers to inquire to know more about Jesus's extraordinarily close relationship with God.

The timing of the crisis was far from ideal. In Capernaum Jesus had revealed himself as the bread of life that came down from heaven. The apostles had not clearly realized what Jesus was saying, but the time had come for them to know.

Peter's Confession of Faith in Jesus

After Capernaum, at Caesarea Philippi, Jesus posed the key questions. "Who do people say that the Son of Man is?" And they said, "Some say John the Baptist, others say Elijah, and others Jeremiah or one of the prophets." He said to them, "But who do you say that I am?" Peter answered, "You are the Messiah, the Son of the living God" (Mt 16:13–17).

"Messiah" is the Hebrew word which means *the anointed one*; in Greek, the translation is "Christ." Anointing refers to solemn placement of consecrated oil on the hair or forehead; in appropriate circumstances, anointing conferred upon a person the status of a priest or king, who was regarded as "the Lord's anointed." This term did not imply divinity. But when Peter confessed his faith in Jesus as the Son of God, he was not speaking symbolically; he was expressing his insight as directly as possible.

After Peter had spoken, Jesus said, "Blessed are you, Simon son of Jonah! For flesh and blood has not revealed this to you but my Father in heaven." Peter had just broken through the momentum of two thousand years of Jewish history, which had properly insisted—against the worship of nature gods—that the human and the divine were distinct and separate. The concept of a human *and* divine Messiah was so new that it had not registered in the minds of the apostles. The insight that Peter proclaimed had come straight from God.

New Truths About Jesus

Jesus's teachings about the bread of life, together with Peter's confession, mark a new phase of the gospel. In this new phase, Jesus could say, "I and the Father are one" (Jn 10:30). This implies that faith and trust in Jesus are equivalent to faith and trust in God as a way to enter the kingdom.

Attending a major feast in Jerusalem, Jesus began boldly teaching in the Temple, challenging his enemies, and proclaiming this to his hearers: "Let anyone who is thirsty come to me, and let the one who believes in me drink. As the scripture has said, 'Out of the believer's heart shall flow rivers of living water'" (Jn 7:37–38). Later he said: "I am the light of the world. Whoever follows me will not walk in darkness but will have the light of life" (Jn 8:12).

We are now prepared to better understand why the Master had referred to himself as the Son of Man. The phrase "a son of man" simply meant a human being. When people speak of Jesus as Son of Man and Son of God, the first title refers to the human Jesus. But Jesus had something else in mind with this title. He was not simply *a* son of man, but *the* Son of Man. He is unique; there is only one. He is the divine human being, in essential ways the pattern for us all (Jn 6:62). We do not literally imitate him, but his life revealed what it means to be a human being, a child of God.

It is common to associate Jesus with the figure in the Book of Daniel called the Son of Man, whose mission is connected with end-of-the-world violence in which God destroys the wicked and upholds the righteous. But those associations are not part of Jesus's teachings. However, it is conceivable that Jesus took this messianic title from the Book of Enoch, which depicts the Son of Man as one who comes down to earth from heaven—which is exactly what he had just proclaimed at Capernaum.

The eternal Son is the Word of God. "In the beginning was the Word, and the Word was with God, and the Word was God" (Jn 1:1). The Son is the one with whom and through whom God created. The teachings that Jesus is the Son of Man, Son of God, one with the Father, the light of the world and the Word of God—all these present a new dimension of the gospel. The gospel is what Jesus taught and more. It is also about who he is. And these advanced teachings give us access to additional insight and motivation.

A Secret for a Time

It was a big surprise to the apostles and a seeming paradox when, after Peter's historic breakthrough, *Jesus "strictly ordered [the twelve] not to tell this to anyone"* (Mt 16:20).

Why should they not immediately proclaim the truth of Jesus's divine Sonship to the crowds? If the Master's real gospel was about being the Messiah and the Son of God, then it made no sense for him to tell the apostles not to proclaim it—unless most of his followers lacked the necessary preparation for this new phase of the gospel. In particular, the twelve needed more time to learn to live and proclaim the riches of the original message.

These considerations raise a question: Why did Jesus lead the apostles into recognizing the higher truth about himself? It was the Father's will. *The world needed to begin to know the fact of Jesus's divine Sonship.* Greatly increased resistance to him and his gospel movement made it timely to use on a new scale his earlier way of responding to "minor" skirmishes. And it meant that Jesus did not have much time left.

As a leader, Jesus was dealing with a very difficult problem. On the one hand, he had to deal with the ongoing conflict that had broken out in Capernaum. After that, there would be more situations to speak sharply to his enemies and about them, and to expand on the truth of his divine Sonship. On the other hand, he needed to keep the movement that he had started on track. But *the cluster of truths surrounding the concept of Jesus as the Son of God were so striking that they could upstage the gospel movement that Jesus had labored to launch during the first part of his public career.* And that is exactly what happened.

The Enduring Validity of the Original Message

It remains a big challenge to receive advanced revelation about Jesus while humbly trusting in Jesus's wisdom: treat higher revelation as truth to be given, ideally, to those who are already established in the saving truth of the original message.

The startling newness and awesome significance of this new cluster of truths makes it important to emphasize that everything in Jesus's basic saving message remains valid. In particular, there was no need for everyone to believe in his divine Sonship in order to be saved. If it were not so, consider the consequences. During the early phase of his ministry, many sincere followers had been welcomed into the kingdom of heaven and had been assured of salvation. But some of them heard nothing of the later, advanced teachings. If their salvation depended on faith in Christ as the Son of God, then they had been deceived. The following teachings are still true.

- The kingdom of heaven still belongs to the poor in spirit, the humble—in other words, those who enter with the faith of a little child. Anxiety about one's own salvation can be left at the door. (Mt 5:3)

- Jesus assured Zacchaeus that his generous repentance had brought him salvation, with no strings attached about his concept of Jesus. (Lk 19:1–10)

- What Jesus said to the rich ruler about what was required for his salvation is still true. If someone who is following the Ten Commandments but still holding on tight to the one thing that is blocking his spiritual progress, then it is enough for salvation to let go of it. (Mk 10:17–27, Mt 19:16–22, Lk 18:18–23)

- What Jesus told the lawyer who asked about eternal life remains true. For salvation, it is enough to love God supremely and the neighbor as oneself. (Lk 10:25–28)

- When Jesus gave his final denunciation of his enemies in the Temple, he exposed their hypocrisy, their failure to live up to their own standards, not their unwillingness to acknowledge him as the Messiah or Son of God. (Mt 23)

All truths of the original message and all truths of the advanced teachings continue to enlighten us without end. And the center of the gospel remains the truth of the family of God.

The advanced teachings do not stand alone as a short cut or alternative to the original message. *To exercise saving faith in Jesus, we need first to understand at least something about his life and teachings.*

When Salvation Requires Belief in the Divinity of Jesus

When we considered what Jesus taught about salvation, it was noted that Jesus did not require faith in him as a necessary condition for everyone wanting to enter the kingdom and family of God. But there is an exception for the situation that some of Jesus's enemies were facing at the pivotal clash in Capernaum: their salvation was at stake.

Some of Jesus's enemies knew him, his teachings, and his actions well enough to have glimpsed his divinity. But they did not face their intuition honestly and allow its implications to change them. Some of them were conspiring to kill him. Their hatred and murderous plotting amounted to sin, deliberate rebellion against God. Therefore, if they were to be saved, they needed to accept Jesus himself as the bread of life.

Note: these same conditions also explain why Jesus responded as strongly as he did even in minor clashes. The same issues of spiritual life and death were surfacing, the alternative of the way of the brittle wineskins of the scribes and Pharisees or the way of the living religion of the spirit.

The turning point at Capernaum was the day when some of Jesus's enemies were making their most important decision. As Joshua had said centuries earlier: "Choose this day whom you will serve" (Jos 24:15). The choice to serve God or not was like a watershed. On either side of the watershed, a river might flow back for a while in the direction of this high ridge; but no river would ever flow across the watershed to the other side.

On this day in Capernaum, the Master expressed love for his enemies by giving them another chance to wake up, turn around, and be welcomed into the kingdom of God. The same teachings also strengthened and protected Jesus's followers. Those who believed were empowered by accepting the revelation of his divinity. It gave them a powerful additional reason for their faith and trust, as well as another layer of security in Jesus as their spiritual refuge.

Transition

Jesus revealed eternity in the trenches of historical developments. He spanned the contrast between divinity and humanity. The human Jesus, our brother, showed how to live as a child of God and a sibling in the family. Jesus, the Messiah, the Christ, the Son of the living God, revealed the fatherhood of God and now revealed himself as divine Son. In proclaiming the full truth about himself, he wanted to add to, and reinforce—not eclipse—his original message.

We have seen some of the higher truths that Jesus proclaimed about himself. The planet has not yet seen what would happen if a critical mass of us were to follow the Master's wisdom, and continue to keep our message centered on the original gospel that Jesus lived and taught. We would then build on that base with advanced teachings for persons who are receptive. To do this effectively, I believe that we need the added insight and power of the higher teachings. We can take a minute to imagine what great good news this program could generate for our world. It would quicken hope for a much better world coming soon.

In the next chapter, we resume our narrative with an account of highlights in Jesus's last week in the flesh. How can he coherently combine messages of peace and militant acts and words?

Questions and Invitations

- Why do you think Jesus wanted to be the only one proclaiming his divine Sonship at the end of his life?

- Do you agree that the advanced teachings tend to upstage the teachings of the original message?

- Do you think that Jesus was wise in getting the original gospel message established before introducing the advanced teachings?

- What practices could help to restore the place of the original message?

- Do you agree that the world might be more receptive to the original message?

19

Forceful Peacemakers

JESUS AND HIS gospel movement were under attack. The Sanhedrin, together with most of the scribes and Pharisees, wanted to exterminate Jesus, his followers, and their teachings. Jesus responded with a spiritual superiority that triumphed over every intellectual and physical challenge that his enemies could muster.

Jesus's Mission of Peace

Isaiah had spoken of the Messiah as the Prince of Peace (Is 9:6–7). Christ began his last, fateful week by entering Jerusalem riding on a donkey. This was a symbolic action, communicating publicly that his mission was one of peace. His action enacted the words of the prophet Zechariah. "Your king comes to you; triumphant and victorious is he, humble and riding on a donkey . . . and he shall command peace to the nations" (Zech 9:9–10).

As Jesus rode the donkey toward Jerusalem, when the Master got close enough to see the city, he wept: "If you, even you, had only recognized this day the things that make for peace! But now they are hidden from your eyes." Jesus knew that the Temple leaders had made up their minds to reject his spiritual leadership and seek his death. The consequences would prove disastrous when Israel engaged in a politically suicidal rebellion against Rome (66–73 CE). The Roman legions surrounded the city, slaughtered inhabitants indiscriminately, and completely destroyed the Temple (Lk 19:41–44, Mt 24:1–2).

Earlier, Jesus had promised: "Happy are the peacemakers, for they will be called children of God" (Mt 5:4, 9). Even during his last week, embroiled in conflict, Jesus has lessons to teach us about peace and happiness. When facing conflict, we can enter into the fray as a one-sided warrior; or we can embrace a spirituality of rising above the world and staying aloof. But Jesus's actions, to which we now turn, illustrate variations of a third way.

Cleansing the Temple for Worship in Spirit and in Truth

By his actions and his teachings, Jesus opened a wide way for people to worship God in spirit and in truth. Forcefully and courageously, he confronted abuses in the Temple where the poor were being exploited. "When it was almost time for the Jewish Passover, Jesus went up to Jerusalem. In the temple courts he found people selling cattle, sheep, and doves, and others sitting at tables exchanging money. So he made a whip out of cords, and drove all from the temple courts, both sheep and cattle; he scattered the coins of the money changers and overturned their tables" (Jn 2:13–15).

Vendors were charging unfair rates to exchange money into the coin in which the Temple tax had to be paid. There were animal pens containing the ritually perfect animals that were sold at high prices for the noisy and bloody sacrifices associated with the Temple rituals of that day. Jesus drove those animals out. His actions disrupted the unholy business in the Temple. However, Jesus only used force in a manner that did not descend into violence. There is no evidence that he injured anyone, stole any money, or destroyed property. His action was intelligently targeted, emotionally controlled, and ethically elegant. On the field of action, in the midst of conflict, he maintained self-mastery and inner peace.

Some people say that in this episode Jesus got angry. But he did not lose control and fly into a destructive rage. If we use his teachings to interpret his life, we can go back to the Sermon on the Mount, where he had condemned anger as leading to murder, like lustful looking leads to adultery. To attribute anger to Jesus is to misunderstand him. What he showed was righteous indignation. Anger is an emotion of the lower nature; righteous indignation is a feeling of the soul. Anger threatens; righteous indignation sees a wrongdoer as a brother or sister and strongly urges the person to come forth from the shadows into the light. Anger is ready to retaliate; righteous indignation does what is necessary without excess.

Jesus did not seek conflict, but when it came to him, he faced it with appropriate force and personal balance. It would have been incoherent for a spiritual peacemaker like Jesus to smile at the murderous scribes and Pharisees who were trying to destroy him and his gospel movement. What Jesus did instead—*non-violent but forceful action*—was fully consistent with his mission of peace.

Additionally, let us recall what Jesus told the Samaritan woman who wanted to know where to worship—Mt. Gerizim or

Jerusalem (Jn 4:23–24). The real issue is to worship God in spirit and in truth: "The hour is coming and is now here when the true worshipers will worship the Father in spirit and truth, for the Father seeks such as these to worship him. God is spirit, and those who worship him must worship in spirit and truth." Authentic worship is not about ritual or geographic location; it is about the true God, personal focus, and sincerity.

To worship in spirit implies, to begin with, that we are sincere, as opposed to paying lip service and going through the motions with our minds somewhere else (Mt 4:10, Lk 4:8, Is 29:13). In true worship, the heart is close to God. Moreover, since God is spirit, we can focus on God's spirit within; and when we are centered on God's spirit, we join all others who are comparably centered. The indwelling spirit of God is our guide into the high country of worship.

To worship in truth means not contradicting the light of the truth that we have received. Recall the Master's wilderness teaching on worship: "Worship the Lord your God, and serve only him" (Mt 4:10). Knowing God both intellectually and personally prepares us for worship. Worshiping in truth implies that what is said, taught, sung, and done should be consistent with truth as we know it.

Worshiping in spirit and truth creates an opening: we can worship not only with those with whom we agree, but also with persons whose theologies and practices differ from ours. In spite of the differences and hostilities between first-century Jews and Samaritans, Jesus's parable of the good Samaritan made it as clear as could be that a Samaritan can be part of what Jesus lived and taught—the religion of the spirit.

A Brotherly Appeal Followed by Powerful Denunciation

Jesus's final teaching in the Temple was direct and forceful. His hearers included friends and enemies. Even then, the Master moved back and forth among denunciation, merciful and peaceful statements, and a fresh expression of his gospel message.

Jesus showed moderation when he observed, "The scribes and the Pharisees sit on Moses' seat; therefore, do whatever they teach you and follow it; but do not do as they do, for they do not practice what they teach" (Mt 23:1–3). In these words, Jesus communicated respect for the office, but not for the practices of the current officeholders.

As noted in chapter 12, in the most direct language, the Master stated what was perhaps his most striking expression of the fatherhood of God and the brotherhood of man: "You are all brothers. . . . you have one Father, who is in heaven" (Mt 23:8, 9). Speaking to enemies as well as friends, Jesus was clearly voicing in its fullness the message of the universal family.

But Jesus also indicted his enemies:

> Woe to you, scribes and Pharisees, hypocrites! For you build the tombs of the prophets and decorate the graves of the righteous, and you say, "If we had lived in the days of our ancestors, we would not have taken part with them in shedding the blood of the prophets." Thus you testify against yourselves that you are descendants of those who murdered the prophets. Fill up, then, the measure of your ancestors . . . so that upon you may come all the righteous blood shed on earth . . . Truly I tell you, all this will come upon this generation (Mt 23:29–36).

Jesus gave a sobering lesson on what it can mean for a religious leader to be held accountable. Those entrusted to lead have a solemn responsibility. Sooner or later, consequences arrive from actions or words that are untrue, ugly, and evil. Accountability is collective, and responsibility spans generations.

In the above denunciation, Jesus did not play the role of a judge. But he could foresee how history would take its course, how his opponents would experience the consequences of rejecting him. While repentant individuals would always find forgiveness, the final decision of the Sanhedrin to have him killed sealed the fate of a nation. Mercy can be repeatedly rejected by a hardened heart. The Sanhedrin failed the crucial test; brittle wineskins rejected the wine of the spirit.

Jesus strongly expressed his desire to save his people: "Jerusalem, Jerusalem, the city that kills the prophets and stones those who are sent to it! How often have I desired to gather your children together as a hen gathers her brood under her wings, and you were not willing!" (Mt 23:37).

Then came his concluding words: "See, your house is left to you, desolate" (Mt 23:38). After that, Jesus left the Temple together with his followers. The years of repeated attempts to win over the religious leaders were over. He made no further critique of his enemies and never came back to the Temple, even after his resurrection. Jesus's participation in the conflict was over.

Deep Peace Can Empower Militant Action

While protecting his gospel movement, Jesus maintained deep peace. His forceful actions were consistent with his teaching, "Happy are the peacemakers, for they shall be called the children of God" (Mt 5:9).

The Son of God had within him a divine quality of spiritual peace that enabled him to be a peace *giver*. If someone with great faith in Jesus was suffering from a troubled spirit, it was as though the Master could say, "Peace, be still," and immediately quiet the storm in the heart of the receptive individual. He said, "My peace I give to you; not as the world gives do I give to you. Let not your heart be troubled, neither let it be afraid" (Jn 14:27). There are many techniques for relaxing mind and body, but Jesus's gift of spiritual peace—which the children of God can pass on to others—is on a higher level.

Jesus's conduct during confrontation is exemplary. The peace of Jesus does not turn a person into a blissful, extreme mystic who, when things get rough, fears conflict, becomes passive on the field of action, and does nothing in the face of evil. Instead, the victories come from returning good for evil.

Jesus, the Prince of Peace, was a remarkable leader. He defended his movement from those who would try to destroy it. But he also tried to wake up his opponents, especially the Temple authorities whose salvation and nation were at stake.

Summary and Transition

Jesus could simply proclaim his mission of peace, as he did when entering Jerusalem. He could be primarily militant, as in his cleansing of the Temple. And he could mix mercy and denunciation, as in his final act of critique. In a particular conflict, whether the divine way calls us into action, bids us remain silent, or some balance of both, we need the foundation of the world-transcending peace that Jesus offered.

His gospel movement was carrying truth which needed to be preserved for future generations. When a movement based on divine ideals is being persecuted by people who are trying to destroy it, love does not smile quietly and do nothing. Jesus protected his movement by a combination of peaceful and uplifting words and deeds—and aggressive and forceful action when required.

Now we turn to Jesus's last day with his followers. It includes his last supper with his apostles and his farewell discourse. On this evening we shall focus on learning the ways of spiritual unity.

Questions and Invitations

- What can we do to receive and give more of the peace that Jesus gives?

- Why does peacemaking (or peacekeeping) require that at times we be forceful?

20

How Jesus Led His Followers into Spiritual Unity

IF FRIENDS ARE going on a trip and we agree to look after their house while they are gone, shortly before their departure, they may have instructions to communicate to us. After they leave, we apply ourselves diligently to do what they told us.

When Jesus gathered with the apostles for their last supper, he knew what was going to happen afterward: arrest, trials, crucifixion, resurrection, and ascent to the Father. During these last precious hours when he was physically present with them, everything that he said and did prepared them to stay connected with him—and with each other. He clarified the meaning of greatness, established the sacrament of the bread and the cup, gave the new love commandment, warned realistically of coming persecution, prayed for his followers' spiritual unity, and taught other essential truths that would help him spiritually lead humankind all the way to our planetary destiny.

The Mark of Greatness

In first-century Palestine, guests would commonly arrive at the home of their host after having walked in sandals on dusty and dirty streets. According to custom, they expected an initial act of hospitality, usually performed by a slave or low-class servant. But no one had done this for the apostles when they arrived at the upper room for their last supper with Jesus. When the Master came in, he took note of this and did what none of them had thought to do. Jesus "took off his outer robe and tied a towel around himself. Then he poured water into a basin and began to wash the disciples' feet and to wipe them with the towel that was tied around him" (Jn 13:4–5). One by one he went around the table, until it was Peter's turn:

> He came to Simon Peter, who said to him, "Lord, are you going to wash my feet?" Jesus answered, "You do not know now what I am doing, but later you will understand." Peter said to him, "You will never wash my feet." Jesus answered, "Unless I wash you, you have no part in what I am doing." Simon Peter said to him, "Lord, not my feet only but also my hands and my head!" Jesus said to him, "One who has bathed does not need to wash, except for the feet, but is entirely clean. And you are clean, though not all of you" (Jn 13:6–10).

To live the life that Jesus showed us includes being ready, as Jesus was, to do humble service to others. Furthermore, to take part in what Jesus was doing, we must also be receptive to being inwardly cleansed by the Master. His statement that "not all of you" are clean refers to Judas, the betrayer.

From time to time the apostles had disputed over who was greatest in the kingdom. Concerning individuals who regard themselves as *better* than others, Jesus had previously said, "The greatest among you will be your servant"; "Those who exalt themselves will be humbled, and those who humble themselves will be exalted" and "Many who are first will be last, and many who are last will be first" (Mt 23:11–12, 19:30). In other words, there is no one greatest member in the family of God. And greatness is not a matter of competing for status or seeking benefits in return. Rather, greatness is attained through high levels of service.

Jesus Is Present in the Sacrament

With their feet washed, the apostles now sat down to supper. At the end of their meal, Jesus distributed bread and wine to establish the new sacrament. Differences over how to interpret these elements have proved to be divisive. My belief is that when the sacrament is taken sincerely by those who believe in the Son, Jesus is present.

He said, "Do this in remembrance of me" (Lk 22:19). To remember Jesus includes recalling something of his life and teachings. In the mystery of the sacrament, we develop oneness with Jesus, whose oneness with the members of the believing community brings us all closer together.

The New Commandment of Love

The commandments of love for God and the neighbor had been prominent in Jesus's original message, but at this last supper, as part of farewell discourse, he gave a third love commandment: "Love one another as I have loved you" (Jn 13:34).

Then the Master made explicit some of the new commandment's implications.

- "No one has greater love than this, to lay down one's life for one's friends."
- "You are my friends if you keep my commandments."
- "I have said these things to you so that my joy may be in you, and that your joy may be complete."
- "By this everyone will know that you are my disciples, if you have love for one another." (Jn 13:34–35, 15:11–12)

Fruitful Branches on the Vine

Jesus again turned to symbols to reveal himself further:

> I am the true vine, and my Father is the vine cultivator. He removes every branch in me that bears no fruit. Every branch that bears fruit he prunes to make it bear more fruit. You have already been cleansed by the word that I have spoken to you. Abide in me as I abide in you. Just as the branch cannot bear fruit by itself unless it abides in the vine, neither can you unless you abide in me. I am the vine, you are the branches. Those who abide in me and I in them bear much fruit (Jn 15:1–5).

To abide means to remain or stay. For us to abide in Jesus means to stay connected with him.

He is in us, and we are in him. We bear much fruit by living in a way that allows Jesus to live through us. "As the Father has loved me, so I have loved you; abide in my love. If you keep my commandments, you will abide in my love, just as I have kept my Father's commandments and abide in his love" (Jn 15:9–10).

Jesus's commandments obviously include the ones in the original message.

The Way to the Father

During this conversation with the apostles, Jesus told them that he would be going to the Father. Then he said one of those things that stretched them, challenged them to expand their understanding: "You know the way to the place where I am going" (Jn 14:4). This statement stimulated Thomas's desire for down-to-earth facts. He asked for clarification and got this reply: "I am the way, the truth, and the life; and no one comes to the Father except through me" (Jn 14:6). Jesus's statement about coming to the Father through him has often been misinterpreted. Some say that every person must explicitly come to believe in Jesus in this life or else be lost forever. But this idea conflicts with his teachings on salvation (chapter 3), so there must be another interpretation that harmonizes these teachings. Many followers agree that spiritually sincere and growing persons who do not know Jesus can have a chance to recognize him after this life. Jesus enables all faithful persons to be fruitful; and he receives into the next life many souls who do not yet know him as a person distinct from God.

The World's Hatred

The Master gave his hearers a frank, realistic warning about the persecution that many of them would face from "the world." This term as I interpret it refers to those whose lives are all caught up in unspiritual concerns. They will be unable to understand persons who come alive in proclaiming truth and who are committed to returning good for evil. The world will feel threatened by such followers and hate them. By the end of the first century, the Roman Emperor Domitian would crucify thousands of believers who refused to call him God.

Jesus said, "I have overcome the world" (Jn 16:33). This implies that the spiritual achievements that he had already gained made certain his triumph over the horrors of the cross. "Let not your hearts be troubled, and do not let them be afraid" (Jn 14:27). As branches on the vine, we can overcome whatever obstacles get in the way of obeying Jesus's commandments. He said to his followers who might be brought before authorities who would persecute them, "Do not worry about how you are to speak or what you are to say; for what you are to say will be given to you at that time; for it is not you who speak, but the spirit of your Father speaking through you" (Jn 14:27, 16:33; Mt 10:19–20).

The Spirit of Truth

Jesus promised to help us after he had returned to heaven by sending the Spirit of Truth, the Comforter, also identified with the Holy Spirit. We have God in us by his spirit within. Now, by means of this Spirit, we also have Jesus in us. This Spirit makes it possible for Jesus to live through us in a new way. The fruitful branches on the vine bear the fruits of the spirit. These are qualities of Jesus, his attitudes, and ways of loving service to all (see the discussion in the first section of chapter 23).

He said that the Spirit of Truth would "lead you into all truth" (Jn 16:13). The well of new and living truth to be revealed cannot dry up. Later generations face new difficulties; and to help his followers meet them, Jesus wants to reveal new truths to enlighten and comfort receptive minds and souls.

This spirit deserves more attention as the Comforter. Another beatitude is relevant: "Happy are they who mourn, for they shall be comforted" (Mt 5:4). Mourning can be for the past, present, or future, and for self or others. Jesus wept over the fate of Jerusalem. He was experiencing understanding compassion for those who would be grieving. Mourning is the spiritual practice of grieving which is mingled with happiness because of present faith in the promise of future divine comfort. The Comforter reveals the friendship of Jesus.

Our Spiritual Unity

While Jesus had concluded the body of his teaching, he had yet more to reveal. In a far-reaching prayer for his followers in every age, the divine Son prayed to the Father, "May they all be one, even as you are in me and I am in you" (Jn 17:21). The oneness he calls for is a kind of mutual indwelling. And Jesus clearly refers not only to his immediate hearers but also to all believers in every generation (Jn 17:20).

Jesus's oneness with the Father does not erase the distinction between them as persons. In the same way, oneness between his followers does not imply the sacrifice of our unique personalities. Just as worshiping in spirit and truth does not imply that all worshipers are to follow the same outward practices, so spiritual unity does not imply that all believers have to think alike.

Jesus prayed out loud so that we could join the prayer and do our part: "May they all be one." The Master anticipated our significant differences, which he does not want to divide us. For thousands of years, Jesus has been nurturing this goal.

Summary and Transition

We can look at what Jesus said and did this evening as the foundation for spiritual unity: service to everyone; the sacrament; the commandment to love as he loved us; the balancing realism of the warning about the world's hatred; and the promise to send the Spirit of Truth, which would enable the life in the vine to flow into and through the Master's fruitful branches. Thus, all his followers are to become one.

These teachings and practices will light the path of humankind all the way to our destiny, when the Father's will shall be done on earth as in heaven. But first Jesus must undergo crucifixion, to which we now turn.

Questions and Invitations

- How can doing humble service for others promote spiritual unity? What kinds of service do you most like to do? Least? Why?

- The new commandment to love as Jesus loves has implications that are little discussed: laying down one's life, Jesus's friends keeping his commandments, our joy becoming complete, and being known by our love as his disciples. Let's ponder these implications.

- When you are at your best, can you feel Jesus living through you?

- Jesus's beatitude on mourning promises happiness and divine comfort. How can the Comforter transform grieving? How can we befriend someone who is grieving?

- How in your experience do the above activities and teachings help make us one? What would you add to this list?

21

How Jesus Interpreted His Death on the Cross

BURNED INTO THE memory of Jesus's followers are scenes from his last hours:

- The agony of his prayers in Gethsemane to gain reassurance that the cross was in fact the Father's will

- His silent dignity in the face of abuse in one trial after another

- Praying to God to forgive the soldiers assigned to carry out the order to crucify him

- Assuring a repenting thief on a nearby cross that he was going to wake up in heaven

- Arranging for John to take care of his mother
- The horror of his suffering

These memories are all linked with Jesus's death on the cross. What does it mean? While there are different interpretations, I propose to center the chapter on Jesus's own words.

Shepherds and Flocks in Ancient Israel

To a great extent, Jesus's view of the cross was given in his parable of the good shepherd. In ancient Israel, shepherds and their flocks were a part of everyday life. People often spoke of God, their leaders, and the people, in terms of shepherds and sheep. A long line of prophets—including Jeremiah, Isaiah, Ezekiel, and Zechariah—compared God to a caring shepherd, or described disastrous leaders in Israel as irresponsible shepherds. As Moses's death was coming near, before he made Joshua his successor, he prayed to God to appoint a leader so that the Israelites would not be "like sheep without a shepherd" (Nm 27:17). The same phrase describes Jesus's compassion for a crowd.

Similarly, Psalm 23 begins, "The Lord is my shepherd"; it goes on to mention how a shepherd takes care of the sheep. "He makes me lie down in green pastures; he leads me beside still waters." "Your rod and your staff, they comfort me." "You anoint my head with oil." Sheep cannot drink fast-moving water; they need still water. For them to flourish takes a great deal of work. Without a shepherd, sheep would have a hard time finding the food and water to survive. The rod and staff are to discipline them and pull them up out of holes and ditches that they fall into. Anointing gives protection from flies that make them miserable.

The shepherd knows them, and they know the shepherd, whose presence allows them to feel peaceful.

If one sheep wanders off and gets lost, it is normal for a shepherd to leave the flock. A lost sheep is in danger of predators and thieves; or it may simply roll over too far and end up on its back with its legs in the air, unable to get back up. Sheep are largely ignorant of what is good for them; when they wander off and get lost, they can panic; and sometimes the herd instinct makes them all follow the one that wanders off, so they all get lost.[31]

With that said, when Jesus referred to his followers as sheep, he did so respectfully, on the basis of over a thousand years of religious tradition and experience in the daily life of the people. Moreover, he was using a term with overtones of affection. The great fondness that one could have for a sheep is portrayed in the parable that the prophet Nathan told to David. It was about a poor man who "possessed only one little female lamb, which he had raised. It grew up with him and with his children; it used to eat of what little he had to eat, and drink from his cup, and lie on his chest, and it was like a daughter to him" (2 Sm 12:1–19).

The Gate to the Sheepfold and the Good Shepherd

Jesus's new commandment that we should love one another as he has loved us (Jn 13:34) takes on new meaning in the light of two of his parables with implications for understanding his death. First, the Master portrayed himself as the gate to the sheepfold—an outdoor enclosure where the sheep come in at night to be safe while they sleep: "I am the gate. Whoever enters by me will be saved, and will come in and go out and find pasture. The thief comes only to steal and kill and destroy. I came that they may have life, and have it abundantly" (Jn 10:1–10). When Jesus told this parable, his hearers were divided between supporters and enemies who were trying to gain access to his disciples and discredit him. Their purpose was to steal his disciples, persecute his followers, and destroy his movement.

Standing against these threats, Jesus identifies himself as the good shepherd:

> I am the good shepherd. The good shepherd lays down his life for the sheep. The hired hand, who is not the shepherd and does not own the sheep, sees the wolf coming and leaves the sheep and runs away—and the wolf snatches them and scatters them. The hired hand runs away because a hired hand does not care for the sheep. I am the good shepherd. I know my own and my own know me, just as the Father knows me and I know the Father. And I lay down my life for the sheep (Jn 10:11–21).

Although none of Jesus's followers can be *the* Good Shepherd, under his leadership, humans can be under-shepherds.

Love Is the Motive

Jesus's supreme motive was clear from what he had said hours earlier: "No one has greater love than this, to lay down one's life for one's friends" (Jn 15:13). To lay down one's life does not imply seeking to be a martyr, throwing one's life away, or playing the role of a passive victim. The goodness of a shepherd's care and the flourishing of the sheep grow out of the fact that he knows them and they know him. Our Good Shepherd knows his followers, and we know him. Out of this mutual knowing grows the motivation to lay down one's life when doing so becomes necessary. Jesus's dominant motive was love and friendship. The cross was not a duty done out of rigorous obedience to a harsh God dominated by concepts of law and justice.

The Master had taught, "Love your enemies" (Mt 5:44; Lk 6:27, 35). He entered Jerusalem, his enemies' stronghold, on a mission of peace and friendship, continuing to offer mercy and salvation. Even when mistreated, his followers are not to give way to the desire for retaliation and vengeance. In the Mediterranean world, it was widely taught that we should do good to friends and harm to enemies. By contrast, the golden rule calls faithful followers to find active, positive, creative ways to return good for evil (Lk 6:27–36, Mt 5:38–48). Jesus passed through the worst his enemies could muster. His bravery and poise are a triumph forever.

In the farewell discourse, the Master expressed his assurance that in his last hours, he would experience joy along with suffering. In the midst of suffering on the cross, by citing the first verse of Psalm 22, Jesus suggests joy by the very words which may seem like a cry of despair: "My God, my God, why have you forsaken me?" (Ps 22:1, Mt 27:46). The first part of the psalm describes the seemingly hopeless situation of a person who is surrounded by enemies and about to be killed. But God acts to save him, and he rejoices greatly; he promises to proclaim his salvation to the congregation, and then immediately starts doing so! The fact that Jesus quoted this psalm makes it likely that he had the whole psalm in mind. And for him to quote this on the cross implies that the psalm is typical of the beatitudes: its promise is not completely fulfilled in this life.

A Culminating Sense of Mission

There was a kind of suffering that was inherent in the very mission of the Son of God to come down from heaven into this dark world. Because the cross was the most intense part of that suffering, it can be the highest symbol of his entire life on earth.

Some of the many features of Jesus's mission include:

- Build on the heritage of Jewish tradition
- Proclaim the gospel message
- Seek and save the lost; call sinners
- Bring life and more abundant life
- Lay down his life for us

Jesus fulfilled his mission by growing up to the maximum of human greatness, proclaiming his message, revealing his divinity, and dealing justly and effectively with his enemies. As the conclusion of his earthly life drew near, his full gospel gained a significant new truth, and his mission acquired a new component: "Now my soul is troubled. And what should I say: Father, save me from this hour? No, it is for this reason that I have come to this hour" (Jn 12:27–28). As I interpret it, this reason implies a new sense of purpose—that in a certain way, laying down his life is what he came into this world to do.

Jesus spoke his last words in a loud voice, expressing triumph and trust: "It is finished. Father, into your hands I commend my spirit" (Jn 19:30, Lk 23:46). Jesus had completed every component of the mission that the Father had given him for his life on earth.

Why the Good Shepherd Had to Die on the Cross

Jesus refused to avoid death. On the cross, he was mocked by people who said, "If you are the Son of God, come down from the cross" (Mt 27:40). He could have done so. The fact that he had the power to do this but refused to use it to save himself makes his death on the cross completely voluntary. In fact, he could have left the planet like the ninth-century BCE prophet Elijah, who is reported to have been taken directly into heaven without passing through death (2 Kgs 2:11). Perhaps Jesus could have accomplished most of the essentials of his mission and gone straight to heaven without having to die. But the Father willed for Jesus to go all the way to the end of the human life. By suffering and dying on the cross, the Good Shepherd became the fully experienced leader for the rest of his followers, no matter what kind of death we might have to face.

Jesus also said, *"If any of you want to come with me, you must forget yourself, take up your cross, and follow me"* (Lk 14:27). As Jesus drew near Jerusalem for the final confrontation, to follow him in the literal sense meant walking into the stronghold of his enemies. For the rest of us, to pick up our cross symbolizes fulfilling our daily responsibilities, especially the ones we find unwelcome.

We Can Prepare Ourselves for Heroic Service

As early as the beatitudes of the Sermon on the Mount, Jesus knew that some of his followers would be persecuted. The Son of Man revealed the heavenly perspective to those who might suffer savage verbal attacks, have lies told to discredit them, or be put to death on account of their fidelity to him.

> Happy are those who are persecuted for the sake of righteousness, for theirs is the kingdom of heaven. Happy are you when people revile you and persecute you and utter all kinds of evil against you falsely on my account. Rejoice and be glad, for your reward is great in heaven, for in the same way they persecuted the prophets who were before you (Mt 5:10-12).

To be ready to find true and real happiness in all the beatitudes is to know the happiness of Jesus. And "perfect love casts out fear" (1 Jn 4:18). By living the complete human life unto death, Jesus led the way for all his followers who would be persecuted, risk persecution, or simply stake their lives by courageous loyalty to him and his message.

Confident in his mission, Jesus knew that his life, message, death, and resurrection would eventually blaze the spiritual trail all the way to abundant living and planetary destiny, no matter how long it might take. In that assurance, he had the vision, calm, and bravery to fulfill all righteousness. In crisis leadership and countless other ways, Jesus was indeed *the* Good Shepherd.

Jesus did not seek to be a martyr; and we do well not to overemphasize readiness to die as a mark of heroic service. Idealism, stamina, resilience, and selfless service in other ways are more common qualities of a hero.

Having said these things, it remains true that Jesus is a paradigm of a hero. In Gethsemane, he made his final decision to fulfill his Father's will that he go to the cross. His decision was to accomplish all righteousness in heroic service for the human race. His willingness to suffer and die for the universal family was an inspiring example for his followers, many of whom have also had to face great difficulties, struggles, and painful death. But if, like

Jesus, we strengthen our relationship with our heavenly Parent and our commitment to serve the family of God well before severe trials are upon us, we improve our chances to follow Jesus into heroic service.

In sum, this chapter completes Part III by portraying Jesus as the Good Shepherd who, for love of his flock, fulfills the Father's mission for him by laying down his life. Having done so, he is fully able to inspire even the most heroic of those who are spirit-led. The next chapter opens Part IV, which begins with the hope of continuing our adventure in heaven, offers a description of what it means to be spirit-filled, and culminates with the hope of a much better world in this century or the next.

Questions and Invitations

- What would it mean for you to think of Jesus as your Good Shepherd? How would it feel? What might you do in response?

- What would it mean for you to "pick up your cross" and follow Jesus? What tasks are yours to carry out? Which of them are the most challenging? Can you believe in Jesus as a friend who works by your side?

Part IV
THE RESURRECTED JESUS CONTINUES HIS WORK THROUGH US

Part IV has just four chapters, shorter than average, designed to expand horizons and encourage hope. They go beyond common ideas. The topics are: resurrection and heaven; what the Spirit poured out at Pentecost does and does not do for us; why it is reasonable to hope for a worldwide moral and spiritual awakening in this century or the next; and an agenda for how to cooperate in working for this hope.

Our spiritual journey began by being spirit-born (chapter 3 on living faith). It continued with becoming spirit-taught (chapter 12 on the living truth of the kingdom of God and the family of God). Next we explored our ordinary difficulties of becoming spirit-led as we followed Jesus through his extraordinary difficulties in Part III. Finally, Part IV gives us an idea of what it is to be spirit-filled. Here we reach the maximum of human likeness to God.

22

Resurrection in This Life and the Next

IT IS NATURAL to be concerned about our own salvation. It is natural to worry at times whether our spiritual growth is progressing far enough and fast enough. And it is natural to wonder what the next life is going to be like. But all three of these concerns can be addressed by experiencing resurrection here and now.

Most of those who had heard Jesus's promises of his resurrection had a hard believing it. Jesus had repeatedly told his followers that he would be killed and then rise from the dead, but somehow it was still a surprise. After the crucifixion, his close followers were in shock. But unusual things started to happen; stories began to circulate. There was fear, disbelief, and a move by the Temple authorities to suppress the truth of what had happened. They heard that Jesus had spoken of rising in three days; so they had arranged for Roman guards to make sure that Jesus's followers would not steal his body from the tomb and claim that he had been resurrected. Early on Sunday morning, while it was still dark, Mary Magdalene and other women went to the tomb to prepare the body more properly for burial. But they found the tomb empty.

As the sun was coming up, the risen Christ appeared to Mary Magdalene, who then left and told some of the disciples. Peter and another apostle went out and verified that the tomb was empty; but they did not yet believe her report of the resurrection. At first, only the women believed. But then there were other appearances, and the reality of the resurrection began to sink in.

Having experienced defeat and gloom, the believers now experienced joy, liberty, and triumph. Christ had said, "I have overcome the world" (Jn 16:33). Now they saw that he had overcome even death. It was a tremendous encouragement to their faith and a possibility offered to all persons who would humbly accept salvation as children of God.

Only One Part of the Good News

The resurrection was so dramatic that it could upstage Jesus's message. But Jesus worked to keep the gospel movement on track by continuing to proclaim his message of the kingdom: "After his suffering he presented himself alive to [the apostles] by many convincing proofs, appearing to them during forty days *and speaking about the kingdom of God*" (Acts 1:3). Thus, even the resurrected Master continued to emphasize the importance of the original message. Unchanged, his message provided the basis for appreciating the fact of Easter, even as Easter placed another exclamation point after the original message.

A New Concept of Heaven

After the resurrection, Christ appeared to many persons and groups. He was both the same and different. On the one hand, continuity with human nature was evident as the Son of Man walked and talked with people. On the other hand, discontinuity was evident as the Son of God passed through locked doors, appeared and disappeared suddenly. Finally, Jesus departed for heaven.

What is heaven like, and where more specifically did Jesus go? First, the Bible describes heaven as a wonderful and beautiful place. "Around the throne is a rainbow that looks like an emerald; in front of the throne, a sea of glass, like a crystal" (Rv 4:3). "They have in heaven a better . . . substance." Heaven is "a better country," where there is "a city . . . whose maker and builder is God" (Heb 11:16, 11:10, 10:34). "No eye has seen, nor ear heard, nor the human mind conceived what God has prepared for those who love him" (1 Cor 2:9).

Second, we are given a revelation of heaven as containing many places. There is a "heaven of heavens" (Dt 10:14, Neh 9:6, Ps 148:4; see 1 Kgs 8:27, 2 Chr 2:6, 6:18).

Third, since Jesus was returning to the Father, he went to what I would call the highest heaven. It appears that some heavenly places are higher than others. The apostle Paul tells a striking story about someone, possibly himself: "I know a person in Christ who fourteen years ago was caught up to the third heaven—whether in the body or out of the body I do not know; God knows. And I know that such a person . . . was caught up into Paradise and heard things that are not to be told, that no mortal is permitted to repeat" (2 Cor 12:2–4).

Why would there be a multiplicity of heavens with some higher than others? Said Jesus, "In my Father's house are many tarrying places" (Jn 14:2). These places are often called "mansions," which means places to stay. If these are not where we stay forever, then we are faced with a fourth possibility: they are transitional stages of life after death.

I propose that our growth continues beyond this life in one world or level of heaven after another. We have been called to be perfect as our Father in heaven is perfect; but none of us leaves this world having attained highest perfection. Simply dying and being resurrected might not instantly transform us into divine perfection. Could it be that in the next life we pick up where we leave off on earth?

Resurrection After Death—and During This Life

In order to make sense of these possibilities of resurrected life, it helps to recognize another one. Before raising Lazarus, the brother of Mary and Martha, from the dead, Jesus said: "I am the resurrection and the life. Those who believe in me, even though they die, will live; and everyone who believes in me will never die" (Jn 11:25–26). In one sense, resurrection is something that happens after death. For anyone in a position to witness it, it would be an observable fact.

But in the spiritual sense, resurrection does not have to wait. In the parable of the prodigal son, the rejoicing father told the older son: "This brother of yours was dead and has come to life" (Lk 15:32). His transformation was a kind of resurrection. In profound spiritual transformation, we can experience heavenly life now in continuity with earthly life. *This is how we know "the resurrection and the life" that Jesus is.*

Additionally, Jesus told the Samaritan woman: "The water that I give will become a spring of water gushing up to eternal life" (Jn 4:14). Later, in the Temple, Jesus said, "Let anyone who is thirsty come to me, and let the one who believes in me drink. As the scripture has said, 'Out of the believer's heart shall flow rivers of living water'" (Jn 7:37–38). As we take this living water into ourselves, we can, even in earthly life, experience the divine life that Jesus offers.

These experiences, tastes of what heaven is like, heal anxiety about whether we are growing fast enough and reassure us about our own salvation. Spiritual joy and liberty help us when we anticipate or go through suffering as individuals or for our world.

We can imagine being present when Jesus resurrected Lazarus. He called in a strong and powerful voice, "Lazarus, come forth!" And we can imagine Jesus calling us by name when we are not living at our best: "_____, come forth!"

In sum, we can rejoice in Jesus's Easter resurrection, and we can know something of the resurrected life now. Jesus's idea of "mansions in the Father's house" makes us want to know more. I believe that our hunger for spiritual knowledge is stimulated by the Spirit that Peter said on Pentecost was "poured out upon all flesh"—all persons (Acts 2:17)—the topic of the next chapter.

Questions and Invitations

- Do you know anyone who has been reborn like the prodigal son? Does this make sense of the idea of being resurrected in this life?

- Does it make sense that the tarrying places in heaven are where we continue our growth toward the perfection of the highest heaven? When you consider this idea, how does it make you feel?

23

What the Spirit Does—and Does Not Do—for Us

JESUS HAD PROMISED that his life would flow into and through us, like life in a vine flowing into the branches and producing fruit. On Pentecost this promise was fulfilled, and this life began to flow into and through us. The Spirit of Truth made Jesus present in us. Now *all of us, in accord with our receptivity, can allow him to live anew through us. Thus, by our active cooperation—by bearing fruit—we reveal Jesus.*

In his farewell discourse, Jesus had promised to send the Spirit of Truth, the Comforter, also called the Holy Spirit. After his resurrection appearances to his followers, Jesus ascended to heaven. The next morning, on the day of Pentecost, believers gathered in prayer. Suddenly they experienced a spiritual presence and power that Peter immediately recognized as the very gift that Jesus had promised. Peter went out and preached to the crowd, and some three thousand souls were baptized.

In his sermon, Peter cited the scripture foretelling that God would "pour out his spirit upon all flesh"—all humankind. This outpouring was a dramatic expansion of what had been the case before. Before Pentecost, the spirit of God had dwelled only in some. As Isaiah declared, "Thus says the high and lofty one who inhabits eternity, whose name is holy: 'I dwell in the high and holy place, and also with those who are contrite and humble in spirit'" (Is 57:15). Since Pentecost, divine spirit has been present in every person. This presence greatly enhances human potential for a planetary moral and spiritual wakening.

Immediately after Peter's sermon on Pentecost, Jesus's followers in Jerusalem lived for a time in spiritual unity:

> They devoted themselves to the apostles' teaching and the fellowship, to the breaking of bread and the prayers. And awe came upon every soul, and many wonders and signs were being done through the apostles.... And day by day, attending the Temple together and breaking bread in their homes, they received their food with glad and generous hearts, praising God and having favor with all the people. And the Lord added to their number day by day those who were being saved (Acts 2:42–43, 46–47).

Fruitful Branches on the Vine

When Jesus introduced the symbol of the vine and the branches and said, "Bear much fruit" (Jn 15:1–8), he did not define the fruit he had in mind. But Paul did specify various fruits of the spirit: "love, joy, peace, patience, kindness, goodness, faithfulness, gentleness, and self-mastery" (Gal 5:22–23). These are qualities of Jesus and the religion of the spirit that he lived—and there are others, which may include the following:

- Down-to-earth, factual, scientific, realistic, practical knowledge, well applied
- Wisdom integrated from human and divine sources
- Decisiveness that integrates awareness of relevant facts and values
- A joyous, good-humored, invigorating, artistic way of living and teaching
- Loving service
- Spiritual power
- The courage to lay down one's life

If I am right, then any quality that we discern in Jesus may be included among the fruit of the spirit.

In addition to receiving the *life* of the vine, we can also "let the same *mind* be in [us] that was also in Christ Jesus" (Phil 2:5). I believe that the blessings that uplifted Jesus's mind are also available to us, for example, the "spirit of wisdom and understanding," and the spirit of worship in which Isaiah delights (Is 11:1–3).

The Spirit of Truth activates the mind and energizes the soul to empower us to develop what our planet needs—sustainable heroism. Several of Paul's writings illuminate this quality: "We boast in our sufferings, knowing that suffering produces endurance, and endurance produces character, and character produces hope, and hope does not disappoint us, because God's love has been poured into our hearts through the Holy Spirit that has been given to us" (Rom 5:3–5). A more general kind of endurance, stamina, is needed in many aspects of life on earth.

As noted earlier, gentleness without strength is weakness. Strength without gentleness is brutality. When we are suffering from severe blows, we may be unable to feel anything of divine gentleness, goodness, or comfort. But Paul could discern the Comforter and see God's purpose at work in our afflictions: "Blessed be the God and Father of our Lord Jesus Christ, the Father of mercies and God of all comfort, who comforts us in all our affliction, so that we may be able to comfort those who are in any affliction, with the comfort with which we ourselves are comforted by God" (2 Cor 1:3–4).

Paul's attitude is based on cosmic insight: "This slight, momentary affliction is preparing for us an eternal weight of glory beyond all comparison, as we look not to the things that are seen but to the things that are unseen. For the things that are seen are temporary, but the things that are unseen are eternal" (2 Cor 4:17–18). When we feel overwhelmed, the phrase "slight, momentary" is enough to remind us of the higher perspective.

To balance the difficulties of heroic endurance, we can reflect further on why the Spirit of Truth was also called the Comforter. The first name suggests that new insight is available for understanding the message as this spirit leads us into all truth. The second name suggests ever-present support and friendship along the way. Since the challenges of growth and service are substantial, progress requires us to stay in touch with our support: divine fellowship, abundant mercy, and generous patience.

What the Spirit of Truth Does Not Do

The two most prominent early leaders, Peter and Paul, had great gifts, accomplishments, wholehearted love for Jesus, and supreme dedication to proclaiming their versions of the gospel. Therefore, the Spirit of Truth could powerfully sustain them in their work. But the Spirit did not edit their theology. In fact, they had a huge clash (Gal 2:11–14). Before long, other serious disputes took place; and the tendency for followers to split into differing camps arose.

The Spirit does not short-circuit God's divinely designed, long drawn-out plan for evolution. Said the Psalmist, "A thousand years in your sight are like a day that has just gone by, or like a watch in the night" (Ps 90:4). There is no rushing the eternal God. Despite our ups and downs, delays and roughness, imperfect creatures are allowed to struggle, make discoveries, and progress. The Spirit lets us make mistakes and learn the hard way, however long it takes. The Spirit honors the wisdom of God's often inscrutable plan of progress. This is true for personal growth, and it is true for the planet as a whole. The Spirit must work with the realities of evolution.

Truth is reality as discovered by science, interpreted by wise philosophy, and revealed in spiritual experience. The Spirit of Truth is no substitute for science or philosophy or reflective spiritual discernment.

Fortunately, we do not have to settle theological questions before we experience the "spring of water gushing up to eternal life"—an experience of Jesus in us (Jn 4:14). The Spirit of Truth helps transform our character, live the truth of Jesus's original gospel, soak in the new and higher truths about Jesus, and follow him through everything. Receiving this living water blesses our entire personality.

In sum, the Spirit that Jesus poured out on Pentecost enables us to stay connected with him in such a way that we bless one another—by being fruitful branches on the vine. The qualities of Jesus's character are available to us who will take the human steps to make these divine gifts truly our own. This mighty Spirit enabled Paul to live through afflictions heroically. The Spirit brings powerful conviction, yet it does not fine-tune the intellect. But when God wants to get something *done*, the Spirit gives us the power to accomplish it.

Since Pentecost, the Spirit of Truth is loose in the world and is able to touch every receptive heart. Sooner or later, it will lead our world into a better age, the topic of the next chapter.

Questions and Invitations

- What fruit of the spirit—spiritual qualities of Jesus—would you like to acquire?

- Do you believe that Jesus is in you through the Spirit of Truth? Can you reveal Jesus? When you are living at your best, is that what is happening?

- Suppose a person has a very strong conviction. Does this prove that the person is right?

- Are you making progress in staying in touch with your support: divine fellowship, abundant mercy, and generous patience? How do you interpret these phrases?

24

Hope for a Much Better World Coming Soon

HAVING RECEIVED so much good from the Son of Man and Son of God, and having spiritual access to the life in the vine of Jesus's outpoured Spirit, the grateful heart asks him, "How can we help you complete your work on earth?"

Jesus's ultimate goal for our world is the glorious destiny for which he prayed to the Father: "Your kingdom come, your will be done, on earth as it is in heaven." I regard this prayer as certain to be realized sooner or later, even if it takes thousands of years. But someday the spiritual idealism surrounding the concept of the universal family of God will become a practical reality.

But could we responsibly hope for and work for a much better world in the near future, perhaps in this century or the next? The problems in our countries and in our world make it understandable that large numbers of people consume dystopian visions in the arts, which portray scenarios of planetary devastation. But could the following parable of Jesus about an individual also describe a nation or a planet?

> Everyone who hears these words of mine and does them will be like a wise man who built his house on the rock. And the rain fell, and the floods came, and the winds blew and beat on that house, but it did not fall, because it had been founded on the rock. And everyone who hears these words of mine and does not do them will be like a foolish man who built his house on the sand. And the rain fell, and the floods came, and the winds blew and beat against that house, and it fell, and great was the fall of it (Mt 7:7).

In trying times, the faithful sons and daughters of God are tested. The image of the rock was one that Moses had used to refer to God (Dt 32:4). Wisdom selects the sturdy foundation of Jesus's teachings and, with his help, begins to discern their meaning. And then wisdom will build—even a new civilization—upon this foundation.

Realistically, spirituality and religion are not the complete answer for social, economic, and political problems. How long it will take to achieve our planetary destiny is uncertain. But a big step in the right direction could occur comparatively soon: a worldwide moral and spiritual awakening.

A Planetary Awakening to Break Through Our Tangle of Problems

Our planet is groaning in the midst of a challenging and dangerous transition. It is struggling to attain a much better future. The present global crisis involves a tangle of interconnected ecological, social, economic, political, and other difficulties. This tangle is made worse in a world where the drive for material progress holds the upper hand, lacking the essential balance of wisdom and spirituality. This kind of civilization leads many to misery. But disillusionment can also motivate people to seek a better way. To move beyond the present confusion and chaos, we need a planetary spiritual renaissance, a new phase of the kingdom of God on earth.

By itself, the moral and spiritual awakening will not solve the tangle of problems. But wise leaders will be able to gain the cooperation needed to deal effectively with the tangle. The sooner this happens, the more disasters we can avoid.

If I am right about this, it is just a matter of time. Through some combination of divine initiative and human effort, the planetary transformation is bound to happen. Human effort alone cannot do it. Procrastinating about taking the human steps, and waiting for God, science, government, and other people to do everything only allows things to get worse. Fortunately, we can already see some individuals and groups living in a distinctly higher way.

One factor that makes it hard to discern planetary readiness for the spiritual renaissance is our ignorance of the progress being made behind the scenes by invisible beings in the universal family who work with God. Their work was recognized by a commander in the Roman army whom Jesus met in Capernaum:

> Now a centurion had a servant who was sick and at the point of death, who was highly valued by him. When the centurion heard about Jesus, he sent to him elders of the Jews, asking him to come and heal his servant. And when they came to Jesus, they pleaded with him earnestly, saying, "He is worthy to have you do this for him, for he loves

> our nation, and he is the one who built us our synagogue."
> And Jesus went with them. When he was not far from the
> house, the centurion sent friends, saying to him, "Lord, do
> not trouble yourself, for I am not worthy to have you come
> under my roof. Therefore I did not presume to come to you.
> But say the word, and let my servant be healed. For I too am
> a man set under authority, with soldiers under me: and I say
> to one, 'Go,' and he goes; and to another, 'Come,' and he
> comes; and to my servant, 'Do this,' and he does it." When
> Jesus heard these things, he marveled at him, and turning
> to the crowd that followed him, said, "I tell you, not even
> in Israel have I found such faith." And when those who had
> been sent returned to the house, they found the servant well
> (Lk 7:1–10; Mt 8:5–10).

In other words, from the highest heaven to the evolutionary realm where we find ourselves, there are countless beings in the heaven of heavens who serve loyally. The centurion perceived not only that Jesus was high in authority, but also that he could give orders that would be obeyed by lower, invisible beings. The universal family includes more than just humans.

Another reason makes it hard to predict planetary readiness to begin the spiritual renaissance. Only a higher being can truly know what human leadership is already in place and what potentials for effective action are waiting in the wings. In this situation of uncertainty, at times, we find ourselves in a group that is making real progress, and we can help to support such an advance. But we would also do well to nurture resilient, positive attitudes in these times where it looks like our world on the whole is going in the wrong direction. If we find ourselves in a situation that is going downhill, what we can do is to slow the decline. If we don't see the planetary awakening in our lifetime, we can keep the torch shining bright as the planet goes through more agony. Thus the light will be ready for the time when a critical mass of people will have learned the hard way. They will get disillusioned and turn around and seek for truth and righteousness. In either case, even as we take seriously the realistic evidence of planetary decline, it is reasonable to hope that we are closer to a spiritual awakening than we realize.

An Inverted Concept of Meekness for Our Planetary Future

Jesus encouraged us to be meek with this promise, "Happy are the meek, for they will inherit the earth" (Mt 5:5). But what did he mean by "meek"? We tend to think of a meek person as someone who lacks self-respect and defers to the slightest wishes of assertive others. But Jesus was not like that. In his strong character, meekness meant deferring to his Father's will: "Not my will but yours be done" (Lk 22:42). This attitude helps us find God's will.

There may be things in the self that obscure our view of God's will. These things include all our desires of heart, soul, mind, and body—even the conclusions of our best thinking and the highest values that we have found in our spiritual life—because God may have something better to reveal to us. To be receptive to new insight, we must, as the saying goes, "let go and let God."

The power of the beatitude regarding meekness arises partly because it builds upon at least two other beatitudes. It calls us to keep both the humility of a child who is poor in spirit, and the hunger and thirst for righteousness. But there is also something new here. The meek will inherit the earth. What this means can be simply expressed: the good guys win. Given enough generations, the meek will prove to be the ones who found the wisdom and power to prevail over their enemies. They do not use the unjust methods of their enemies, but they are willing to use force.

Those who set themselves in opposition to the kingdom of God weaken themselves in the long run by cosmic foolishness. They indulge desires for personal power and control and make it a habit to be selfish and do evil in God's universe, which is designed to promote goodness.

Meek persons exercise their virtue in situations that affect who controls the planet. Meek persons are willing to work for a much better world, even if they do not see much progress in their lifetime. The best example of strong meekness is Jesus. We have seen how he handled the conflict at Capernaum. He had no evil intent like some of his enemies, but he took charge of the situation effectively. And we have witnessed his cleansing of the Temple and, ultimately, his willingness to accept the cross in order to gain a spiritual triumph for his followers and the world.

In sum, the tangle of planetary problems requires planetary transformation if we are to attain our destiny established by the Creator. Therefore, sooner or later it must occur. There are any number of invisible beings who are helping now. They are loyal to Jesus and his promise regarding the future of our world. Those who are meek in receptivity to God's will are going someday to inherit the earth. Happy in this faith, we look to the next chapter's agenda for accomplishing this.

Questions and Invitations

- Do you believe that our planet will one day realize a glorious destiny? That God's kingdom will come in fullness, and his will shall be done on earth as in heaven? That Jesus's kind of meekness implies that eventually the good people win?

- Do you believe that it is possible for divine and human cooperation to bring forth a new phase of the kingdom of God in this century or the next? That Jesus has the power to order invisible beings to do surprising things?

- What do you find hopeful in our world? How do you cooperate with God in contributing to it? *Are you ready to join in if the time for the spiritual renaissance to get powerfully underway comes in your lifetime?*

25

Jesus and His Gospel: The Agenda

WHAT SPIRITUAL AND religious agenda will best promote planetary progress to the next phase of the kingdom of God? I propose the following. First, the full gospel that Jesus lived and taught must be understood, lived, and proclaimed again—the original message and the advanced teachings where appropriate. Second, the various groups of Jesus's followers are to come together in spiritual unity. Third, we need to lovingly, understandingly, serve non-Christian persons in the wider family of faith—and to serve *with* them. Fourth, divine and human cooperation operates to bring about a spiritual renaissance.

This agenda needs some explanation and support.

Jesus's Original Message Front and Center in Evangelism

The traditional Christian gospel of salvation by faith in the risen Savior has so much truth in it; it has done so much good; and those who have proclaimed it by their lives and their teachings have brought so much divine love, mercy, ministry, and salvation to people, that their work will undoubtedly continue and bear fruit.

But this gospel was not what Jesus lived and taught. Are we ready to imagine the possibility that his original message will sometime do even greater things? A major goal is to *help Jesus get his gospel movement back on track. His good news shall be front and center in our lives and in our spiritual communications with the world. This gospel can go places where the traditional gospel cannot go and do things that it cannot do.*

This conviction of mine has a long history. As noted earlier, during the eighteenth and nineteenth centuries, some scholars in France and Germany began to use historical tools to discover Jesus's real gospel. Some of them concluded that it centered on a pair of truths: the fatherhood of God and the brotherhood of man. By the late nineteenth and early twentieth centuries, this pair of teachings started to show its spiritual power. Moving into the wider society, the gospel movement came to life and spread like wildfire. Here and there around the world, sparks landed among teachers, preachers, and social reformers; most of those ignited were people in non-religious occupations.

We need *new spiritual teachers* to find creative and spontaneous ways to live and proclaim the original gospel. *They need to do so in ways that are courageously faithful to what Jesus revealed about God and wisely sensitive to the language of the people they communicate with.* They will dare to trust the Master's wisdom about what teachings are generally appropriate for beginners and what teachings are added to that foundation.

Directions to the Reunion

The next item on the agenda I do not regard as necessary for a spiritual awakening. But I believe that it must eventually occur and therefore will happen sooner or later. If it happened soon enough, it would tremendously enhance the hope of a much better world soon.

The ideal path to the spiritual renaissance includes the fulfillment of Jesus's prayer for his followers: "May they all be one" (Jn 17:21). Note: the Master did not intend for us to suppress our differences as unique personalities. He never tried to standardize our thinking, feeling, and doing. The unity I am proposing is *spiritual* unity, not any other kind of union. Lacking this, the family of his followers is presently divided into many families. This is the basic reason that we need a family reunion.

In one of Jesus's sociological observations, he warned: "A kingdom divided against itself is laid waste. And no city or house divided against itself will stand" (Mt 12:25, Mk 3:24). Division is dangerous because it weakens our response to challenges and opportunities. Today we confront a secularism that is increasingly aggressive. In some places, especially in the northern hemisphere, Christianity is in decline. Increasingly, young people regard it as stale and hypocritical. People seeking wisdom for daily living often turn to Eastern philosophies, religions, and practices. When faith is weak, it discredits itself, and people fall away. Shall we assume that Christianity, which is only two thousand years old, is exempt from Jesus's warning that division makes groups vulnerable?

Sometimes an attitude of superiority infects a group of believers in Jesus in their attitude toward another group. Even if such feelings are not publicly expressed, the shadows can creep into the heart. Another factor that can eclipse spiritual unity is mixing religion with politics or cultural issues. In the seemingly impenetrable tangle of global problems, one of the biggest difficulties is fierce polarization over what is to be done. I remember a billboard that said, "Real Christians *love* their enemies." Learning to love our opponents is a big step in the right direction.

In his day, the Son of Man dealt creatively with challenges to spiritual unity. He knew the pride of Jews at that time in their relations with Samaritans. He sparked a Samaritan revival at Jacob's well and created the parable of the good Samaritan. During the first phase of his public career, he knew the antagonism of the religious leaders—and responded with a positive message full of joy and welcome that built on the best of Jewish tradition.

The idealistic goal of a family reunion may seem unrealistic, but there are reasons to believe that it can be achieved.

- Though increasing numbers of persons do not identify with any religion, many believe in God, and many of these are open to Jesus.

- In many places around the world today, relations between different families of Jesus's followers are friendly. They take little notice of the differences.

- Some methods of social psychology have gained instructive successes. Techniques of compassionate communication have brought harmony to groups of Palestinians and Israelis, gangs in Los Angeles, gangs and police in Chicago, and countless couples on the verge of divorce. Long-time enemies can achieve mutual understanding and demonstrate this to each other's satisfaction. This achievement leads to extraordinary breakthroughs, which greatly facilitate cooperation on the practical level of what needs to be worked out.[32]

- Ecumenical cooperation encourages me in believing that differences in beliefs and practices will pose no obstacle when believers come together to (1) pray and listen for God's guidance and (2) support one another in sharing Jesus's message as they understand it with their congregations and neighborhoods.[33]

- Differing groups of followers can discover strengths that complement their own. And these strengths overlap. We cherish central values in common and bring forth some of the same fruit of the spirit. The vine is one. Building on the unity that is already there and learning from each other's strengths, the power grows. Yes, we will continue to step on each other's toes; but our reactive nature will be massaged and tempered by tolerance, forgiveness, resilience, and love.

- On the level of soul, the followers of Jesus can be alike. Branches on the vine can join in love, mercy, and service.

Therefore, in the light of these factors, on the basis of our knowing Jesus and understanding his message, I propose this recipe for the family reunion—spiritual unity.

- We believe in the possibility of spiritual unity for the followers of Jesus, commit to it, pray for it, and rejoice, trusting that, sooner or later, it will occur. And we work for it to come soon.

- When persons unite in wholehearted commitment to the will of God, the spirit within helps us grow and gives us the power to keep our differences from dividing us.

- We cooperate by cultivating habits of spiritual unity with members of diverse families of followers of Jesus—Orthodox, Catholic, Protestant, and none of the above.

- Our goal is to love and serve God, one another, and everyone else.

When we attain spiritual unity, others will take a closer look to learn from us. There's a song, "They will know we are Christians by our love." Jesus put it this way: "*By this everyone will know that you are my disciples, if you have love for one another*" (Jn 13:35).

Sooner or later, we will unite and rise above antagonisms. 'Plan A' is for the family reunion to break out soon enough and spread far enough to enhance the hope of a global moral and spiritual awakening, which would prevent some of the worst-case scenarios of our global future.

Ever since Jesus prayed, "May they all be one," he has been nurturing our spiritual unity by seeking persons who will enter into that prayer with him and do their part. How much longer will we make him wait?

The Family of Faith

Our commitment to the universal family should surely make us glad to be part of the wider family of faith—persons of other religions whose lives are being transformed by their faith in God (or a functionally equivalent concept such as Krishna or Amida

Buddha). For that matter, there are persons who are unconsciously in touch with the spirit within, and who do the will of God.

Current statistics claim that there are more than two billion Christians on the planet, mingling with over five billion non-Christian neighbors. For the spiritual awakening to change the world, we will need to love and serve members of other religions. Christians do not have a monopoly on truth. Nor do we have a monopoly on Christ. To be good neighbors, we can affirm our common humanity, learn to understand our differences and similarities, and seek to appreciate the unique personality of each sibling we are privileged to get to know.

Some kingdom believers are excellent neighbors with persons of other religions. They avoid the easy path of contrasting the best of Christian ideals with the worst in the history of other traditions. They inform themselves about other religions' teachings and practices that overlap with those found in the Bible. They include God, the spirit within, love and compassion, the golden rule, prayer and worship, and hope for an afterlife in heaven. It helps to put more emphasis on what we have in common.

Consider how Jesus related with Jewish tradition. His original message did not include truths that cluster around the theme of his being the Son of God; neither did his final teaching in the Temple. Until the clash at Capernaum, he met his hearers on common ground.

The interfaith dialogue movement has evolved a culture in which participants normally approach each other with an attitude of kindness and respect—plus interest in listening to and learning from each other. In these gatherings, I have been struck by meeting many persons of other religions who were bearing fruit of the spirit. I have been inspired and edified by their realization of God's spirit within, their love, their sensitivity to human need, their service, their devotion to the will of God, and their balanced character. I've found that dialogue can be eye-opening. And for unifying the family of faith, *doing* things together is even more powerful.

My world religions course always concluded with the unit on Islam. The students' third project was to have a conversation for at least thirty minutes with a Muslim. I taught principles of interreligious dialogue; but they were not to attempt dialogue in the full sense. Instead, the assignment was to facilitate the other person's expression of their experience of being a Muslim. Most of the conversations ran much longer than the minimum time; and it was common for genuine friendship and appreciation to sprout. Many students had already had transformative experiences in earlier projects; but in the course evaluations, most students reported that the most transformative thing they experienced all semester was the conversation with the Muslim.

The Ideals of Spirit-Filled Living

Parts I–IV trace a development of spirituality that I believe Jesus completed by his baptism: he had become spirit-born, spirit-taught, spirit-led, and spirit-filled. I assume that there are thousands of persons who have attained this highest level. I also suppose that some of them do not think of themselves as followers of Jesus. So what can it mean to be spirit-filled?

I think that the number-one clue to an answer is that all spirit-filled persons are spirit-born, spirit-taught, and spirit-led. This implies that, at the highest level, most of the qualities that we have highlighted in Parts I–III are taken to higher levels and unified more perfectly.

For example, a strong, well-balanced character centered in God becomes stronger, the balance is wiser, and being centered in God is based on an ever-increasing realization of our Parent. And I say with a smile that the balance includes living spontaneously and abundantly in joy and liberty, so that tastes for individuals become a shared feast.

Furthermore, in spirit-filled siblings, by definition, all aspects of life are brought under the sway of spirit. There is no room for an exception. We have seen the standard of participating righteously in family and school, work and play, and in the religious community. But our opportunities in these areas are unequal; and we can only choose among options we know about, such as being aware of the religious questions posed by the agenda of this chapter. So divine fairness perhaps adjusts to the individual in some way what it means to be spirit-filled. Nevertheless, people who are cooperating with God in their transformation discover new frontiers for growth until they attain a certain indefinable human completeness—like the human Jesus did.

The core of what it means to be spirit-filled is that such persons are given the advanced tasks and enjoy the exquisite companionship of a more or less continuous spiritual awareness of God and divine values. This does not mean around-the-clock focusing on God. But they are never far from God. They surpass people on the first three spiritual levels in loving God with all their heart, mind, soul, and strength, and loving each neighbor in a way that is intelligent and wise. Finally, I believe that those who are spirit-filled can learn best how to reveal the Father like the human Jesus did, and how to reveal Jesus by living in such a way that Jesus can live through them.

An Agenda of Hope

On the path from spirit-born to spirit-filled, we have gained a fresh view of Jesus from birth to death and beyond; and we have unfolded a new understanding of his original message and full gospel. Jesus's abiding Spirit presence and his life and teachings guide us in daily life and in these times of great planetary distress. In general, they help us flourish increasingly as members in our Father's universal family. Specifically, they point to a secure long-term framework and a near-term future for which there is great hope.

First, the long-range perspective. From the beginning, our world has been in the hands of the Creator. Also, for two thousand years, Jesus has blessed us through his Spirit of Truth. With God, Jesus is in charge of our planetary destiny, and he gives eternal life to all who will receive it. Having this assurance, we can live more effectively in the present.

Now the near-term picture. It is plausible that each goal of the following agenda will be accomplished sooner or later. The great hope is that the agenda is completed sooner—in this century or the next. So let us envision four imperatives. Help Jesus get his gospel movement back on track by putting his original message front and center in our lives and our spiritual communications with the world. Seek spiritual unity among all groups of Jesus's followers—East and West, North and South, right and left. Cooperate with persons of other religions as equals in the family of faith. And follow Jesus beyond the present chaos and confusion into a spiritual renaissance that will usher in the next stage of the kingdom of God.

The Master's revelation is not over. His Spirit of Truth is leading us into all truth. Each of us can pray for the next layer of truth that God knows we are capable of receiving. Every day we can benefit from a new layer. Let's seek it, expect it for ourselves and each other, and rejoice in advance.

Happy deciding and doing!

Acknowledgments

It is a pleasure to acknowledge my indebtedness to a few persons who have been especially helpful during the decade of my work on this book plus a unique source of inspiration. Rev. Dick Clewell was the prophetic preacher who called me to write it. For five years, Rev. Dr. David A. Palmer was my Bible teacher.

Byron Belitsos was my highly engaged and inspiring publisher at Origin Press. As a lifetime friend, he has supported this project almost since its inception.

I am grateful for comments on parts or all of this book from Stephen G. Post, Ed Owen, Susan Owen, Jonathan Dodson, William Wentworth, and Mahtab Tehrani. Additional support came from Jasmina Tadic, James Blessing, The Rev. Mary Blessing, and my brother, Tom Wattles.

A Taste of Joy and Liberty is inspired by the grand project for the future of Christianity advocated in *The Urantia Book* beginning on page 2086 (Paper 195, section 10). Those familiar with this unique book will see its pervading influence on my ideas about Jesus.

The cover design was created by Ian Noviak and project manager Alan Hebel at bookdesigners.com.

Further Reading

Brown, Raymond E. *The Gospel According to John.* 2 vols. Doubleday, 1966 and 1970.

Finlan, Stephen, and Kharlamov, Vladimir, eds. *Theōsis: Deification in Christian Theology*, vol. 1. Princeton Theological Monographs 52. Pickwick, 2006.

Fredrickson, Barbara. *Positivity: Top-Notch Research Reveals the 3–1 Ratio That Will Change Your Life.* Three Rivers Press, 2009.

Keller, Philip. *The Shepherd Trilogy: A Shepherd Looks at the 23rd Psalm, A Shepherd Looks at the Good Shepherd, A Shepherd Looks at the Lamb of God.* Marshall Pickering, 1996.

Kharlamov, Vladimir, ed. *Theōsis: Deification in Christian Theology*, vol. 2. Princeton Theological Monographs 156. Pickwick, 2011.

Oord, Thomas Jay. *Pluriform Love: An Open and Relational Theology of Well-Being.* SacraSage Press, 2022.

Reese, Martha Grace. *Unbinding the Gospel: Real Life Evangelism.* 2nd edition. Chalice Press, 2008.

Rosenberg, Marshall. *Nonviolent Communication: A Language of Life.* 3rd edition. PuddleDancer Press, 2015.

Tatum, W. Barnes. *In Quest of Jesus.* Revised and enlarged edition. Abingdon Press, 1999.

The Urantia Foundation. *The Urantia Book.* Urantia Foundation, 1955.

Wattles, Jeffrey. *The Golden Rule.* Oxford University Press, 1996.

Wattles, Jeffrey. *Living in Truth, Beauty, and Goodness: Values and Virtues.* Cascade Books, 2016.

Endnotes

1. Quotations from the *Bible* typically use the New Revised Standard Version Updated Edition, unless otherwise noted.
2. Wikipedia, "Babylonian Captivity," Wikimedia Foundation (2025), en.wikipedia.org/wiki/Babylonian_captivity.
3. In the Book of Isaiah, scholars regard chapters 1–39 to be the work of an eighth-century BCE prophet, 40–55 by an anonymous sixth-century prophet, and 56–66 by either Second Isaiah or one or more later prophets. See *The New Oxford Annotated Bible, 5th ed.* (Oxford University Press, 1979 2018), 977.
4. William H. McNeill, *A World History*, 3rd ed. (Oxford University Press), 59–74; see Wikipedia, "Samaritans," Wikimedia Foundation (2025), en.wikipedia.org/wiki/Samaritans.
5. See Martin Albl, *Essential Guide to Biblical Life and Times* (Saint Mary's Press, 2009).
6. See relevant entries on Encyclopedia.com.
7. Jean-Pierre Isbouts, *In the Footsteps of Jesus: A Chronicle of His Life and the Origins of Christianity, 2nd ed.* (National Geographic, 2017), chapters 1–3.
8. An influential model of developmental psychology, set forth by Erik H. Erikson, presented eight stages in the life cycle, in each of which we ideally gain a particular strength. In the first year of life, the most important is trust. See for example his "Eight Ages of Man" in *Childhood and Society* (W. W. Norton, 1950).
9. The quotations are found in the Hindu Bhagavad Gita 2.18–25, 6.47, 9.29, 18.61; the Buddhist Mahaparinirvana Sutra; the Confucian Mencius 4B14; and Guru Nanak, the founder of Sikhism, quoted in W. H. McLeod, *Sikhs and Sikhism* (Oxford University Press, 1984), 174–75.
10. For centering prayer, I adapted the practice of Thomas Keating, *Open Mind, Open Heart: 20th Anniversary Edition* (Continuum, 2006). For conscious breathing I drew on Thich Nhat Hanh, *Peace Is Every Step: The Path of Mindfulness in Everyday Life*, ed. Arnold Kotler (Bantam Books, 1991), 8–10.
11. For this quick summary of early childhood development I used Harvard University Center on the Developing Child, "InBrief: The Science of Early Childhood Development" (2007), developingchild.harvard.edu/resources/inbrief-science-of-ecd/. I think that the stages mapped out by Jean Piaget and Erik Erikson are helpful.
12. John Dominic Crossan, *The Historical Jesus: The Life of a Mediterranean Jewish Peasant* (HarperCollins, 1991), 18.
13. The paragraph on ancient science is one of the places where, I am finding, the labor of creating a nice mix of broadly accessible and academically

helpful endnotes, however fascinating and educational, is not justified by its contribution to the argument of this book.

14 Daniel Kahneman, *Thinking, Fast and Slow* (Farrar, Straus, and Giroux, 2011), 3.

15 A house divided is described in scientific detail in Bradley Wilcox et al., *Why Marriage Matters: Thirty Conclusions from the Social Sciences, 3rd ed.* (Broadway Publications, 2011).

16 Popular presentations of psychological research can complement spirituality, for example, Ali Abdaal, *Feel-Good Productivity: How to Do More of What Matters to You* (Cornerstone Press, 2023).

17 I quote this student by permission, and honor her choice that I not reveal her name.

18 Jeffrey Garcia, "Jesus and His Pilgrimage Practices," Biblical Archaeology Society Library (2021), library.biblicalarchaeology.org/department/jesus-and-his-pilgrimage-practices/.

19 On the Sanhedrin, see Rabbi Aryeh Kaplan, "The Jewish Court System," AISH (2024), aish.com/48936377/.

20 See W. Bradford Wilcox et al., *Why Marriage Matters: Thirty Conclusions from the Social Sciences, 3rd ed.* (The Institute for American Values, 2011), and Robert Capon, "Bed and Board," in Amy Kass and Leon Kass (eds.), *Wing to Wing, Oar to Oar: Readings on Courting and Marrying* (University of Notre Dame Press, 2000), 594–612.

21 Two professors in the Stanford Graduate School of Business have studied, taught, and published a book on, humor. Jennifer Aaker and Naomi Bagdonas, *Humor, Seriously: Why Humor Is a Secret Weapon in Business and Life (And how anyone can harness it. Even you.)* (Crown Currency, 2021).

22 The widespread distinction between an allegory (whose symbols imply many points) and a parable which teaches a main point is set forth in W. Barnes Tatum, *In Quest of Jesus* (Abingdon Press, 1999), 193–96.

23 The Stoic philosopher Cleanthes's Hymn to Zeus illustrates the height of the evolution of the concept of Zeus.

24 This report of Rebecca Jackson is found in Elizabeth A. Johnson, *She Who Is* (Crossroad, 1993), 170.

25 Barbara Fredrickson, *Positivity* (Three Rivers Press, 2009), 39–48.

26 Joshua Mark, "Luther's Speech at the Diet of Worms," *World History Encyclopedia (2021)*, worldhistory.org/article/1900/luthers-speech-at-the-diet-of-worms/.

27 The love of enemies, especially as implied by the golden rule, was central in the theological and philosophical books of Olivier du Roy: *La Réciprocité: Essai de morale fondamentale* (Éditions de l'Épi, 1970), 1–49; *La règle d'or: Le retour d'une maxime oubliée* (Les Éditions du CERF, 2009), 119–34; *La règle*

d'or: Histoire d'une maxime morale universelle, 2 vols (Les Éditions du CERF, 2012), 1:143–64. On the policy of helping friends and harming enemies, see Albrecht Dihle, *Die Goldene Regel* (Vandenhoeck & Ruprecht, 1962).

28 For the theme of the love of enemies and the golden rule generally, I am greatly indebted to the works of French scholar Olivier du Roy, esp. La règle d'or: histoire.

29 The great challenge to evangelism as proclamation is William J. Abraham, *The Logic of Evangelism* (Eerdmans, 1989). Abraham argues that evangelization involves several phases to integrate the new believer into the Christian community.

30 See Marshall B. Rosenberg, *Nonviolent Communication: A Language of Life, 3rd ed.* (Puddle-Dancer Press, 2015); Edwin H. Friedman, *A Failure of Nerve: Leadership in the Age of the Quick Fix* (Seabury Books, 2007); and Hugh F. Halverstadt, *Managing Church Conflict* (Westminster/John Knox Press, 1991).

31 For this information on sheep, I rely on Phillip Keller, *A Shepherd Looks at the Good Shepherd*, in *The Shepherd Trilogy* (Marshall Pickering, 1996).

32 See Rosenberg, *Nonviolent Communication.*

33 See Martha Reese Grace, *Unbinding the Gospel: Real Life Evangelism, 2nd ed.* (Chalice Press, 2008), 31–36 and 41–56.

List of Abbreviations

The Old Testament

Chr	Chronicles
Dt	Deuteronomy
Ex	Exodus
Ezek	Ezekiel
Gn	Genesis
Is	Isaiah
Jer	Jeremiah
Jos	Joshua
1 Kgs	1 Kings
Lv	Leviticus
Mal	Malachi
Neh	Nehemiah
Nm	Numbers
Prv	Proverbs
Ps	Psalm
1 Sm	1 Samuel
Zech	Zechariah

The New Testament

Acts	Acts of the Apostles
1 Cor	1 Corinthians
Eph	Ephesians
Gal	Galatians
Heb	Hebrews
Jn	John
Lk	Luke

Mk	Mark
Mt	Matthew
2 Pt	2 Peter
Phil	Philippians
Rom	Romans
Rv	Revelation

Bible Translations

ESV	English Standard Version
NIV	New International Version
NKJV	New King James Version
NLT	New Living
RSV	Revised Standard Version
NRSVUE	New Revised Standard Version (Updated Edition)
RSV	Revised Standard Version